Avatar Art

NEO-VEDIC PAINTINGS CELEBRATING LIFE

Steven J. Rosen
Kaisori Bellach

THE BHAKTIVEDANTA BOOK TRUST

contents

Mark Arian
(Muralidhara Dasa)
*Krishna Greets His
Parents* (detail),
1983, oil on canvas,
210 × 305 cm

Preface

Avatar – from the Sanskrit: "Descent; a deliberate descent of a deity to earth; a descent of the Supreme Being."

With the proliferation of video games and graphic novels in search of unique characters and storylines, people are becoming more and more familiar with words like *avatar* and *Vedic* and names like Indra, Kali, Krishna, and Rama – all drawn from the rich history and sacred literature of India.

Avatar Art: Neo-Vedic Paintings Celebrating Life offers you a who's who of many of the most popular figures in the Indian mythos. The paintings are contemporary illustrations of gods, devas, demons, sages, and avatars. Learn why Vishnu has four arms, Shiva dances, and Ganesh sports the head of an elephant. Read about the curse that created a snake-bird and led to a king's immolation, and the dishonorable treatment of a queen that ignited the famous *Mahabharata* war. On these pages, Rama and Ravana battle it out, and the man-lion, Narasingha, protects a prince.

For your convenience, *Avatar Art* is divided into three sections. The first, "Avatars, Devas, Sages, and Demons" draws almost all of its imagery from the *Srimad-Bhagavatam*. Most of the personalities we associate with Indian imagery were introduced to the West through this text.

The second section shows the life of Krishna, the playful, blue-skinned deity, drawing mainly from the *Srimad-Bhagavatam,* but also from the *Mahabharata* and other sources.

The final section is filled with images of Sri Chaitanya and his associates. Known as "the Golden Avatar," Sri Chaitanya was a sixteenth-century "descent" of Krishna.

Note: Names of personalities who have their own spreads somewhere in the book are set in **bold** the first time they are mentioned in other spreads. This is to make cross-referencing easier for those who would like to read further about any particular personality.

Vlad Holst (Vasupriya Dasa)
Prabhupada, 1994, oil on canvas, 89 × 68 cm,
Private collection, Stockholm, Sweden

Introduction

STEVEN J. ROSEN

Avatar Art: Neo-Vedic Paintings Celebrating Life is a book of sacred images from the bhakti, or devotional, tradition of yoga. Sacred art is meant to open for both artist and viewer a connection between the world we perceive in three dimensions and the world of spirit. It's art as yoga and yoga as art.

Yoga literally means "to link" or "yoke" one's consciousness with the Supreme consciousness, and bhakti yoga in particular links to the Supreme in a mood of love and service. Some yogis create this link through their asana practice or by chanting mantras or by meditating; others paint. This book contains the revelations received by thirty-one bhakti artists as they illustrate the *Srimad-Bhagavatam* and other sacred Indian texts in a mood of meditation.

Studying under masters in the sacred bhakti lineage and molding their lives accordingly, these artists dedicate their lives to depicting the message of transcendence.

Bhakti Art

For a person engaged in bhakti yoga, *rasa* is the soul of art. It's beyond the scope of this book to give a complete analysis of *rasa* and its place in either aesthetics or spiritual practice, but here are a few simple definitions of the word: "juice," "essence," "savor," and "that which creates resonance" in the relationship between artist, composition, and viewer. *Rasa,* one might say in the present context, is both the emotional content of a piece and how the piece communicates with those who see it. *Rasa* comes into being due to an artist's emotional engagement to a particular subject, as well as in his or her ability to convey that emotional engagement with the viewing audience. In terms of bhakti, all emotions refer to the various flavors of love that are found in God's relationships with his numerous devotees.

Rasa, like love, is often subtle, expressed

Rasa is both the emotional content of a piece and how the piece communicates.

with nuance and suggestion rather than overtly stated. We know of its presence through incidental things – in painting, we may perceive *rasa* through symbols, distinct style or the choice of colors. When a piece "has *rasa*" – and if the viewer is spiritually sensitive enough, because after all, *rasa* involves communication – the piece becomes a bridge between artist and the divine, artist and viewer, and the divine and the viewer, allowing for each to taste or experience the emotions of the other. Art, then, becomes a mystical experience, allowing one to enter the transcendent world of the scene being depicted.

This is why bhakti yogis claim their art can give one direct access to God and his kingdom. Their art is not merely representational; it is mystically nondifferent from spiritual substance, although formed of what might ostensibly be considered material elements. When art is infused with the artist's intent to

love God and enlighten others, and when it is guided by those already experienced in love of God, bhakti art can literally depict and convey the divine.

Why the need for guidance? Bhakti yogis, like those on most spiritual paths, think it offensive to concoct spiritual images. They are not interested in exploring their imagination, but, instead, seek revelation. They also try to steer clear of hubris; they don't assume that whatever vision they may have of God is in fact God or the complete truth. That's why bhakti-inspired artists necessarily derive their imagery from sacred texts, particularly works like the *Srimad-Bhagavatam,* which describe God's numerous forms and his kingdom in detail. While the sacred texts of other traditions may tell us of God's greatness, they don't reveal details of his personality and form. The *Srimad-Bhagavatam,* however, paints in poetic verse the beauty of God's many forms and the

Pieter de Grebber
God Inviting Christ to Sit on the Throne at His Right Hand (detail), 1645, oil on canvas, 115 × 133 cm, Museum Catharijneconvent, Utrecht, The Netherlands

forms of his eternal associates. It also describes the personified, if subtle, forces that rule the mundane world, both good and evil, as well as the terrain – the mountains, caves, forests, and rivers that occupy God's kingdom and the worlds beneath it. This information affords bhakti artists a truly unique opportunity.

In fact, whenever any artist attempts to depict the divine, he or she must choose from one of three approaches: (1) to convey him as an abstraction, with no form, perhaps suggesting spirituality with color and mood; (2) to show how the sacred pervades nature, either by highlighting the beauty of the natural world or by more literally showing how God exists in the creation; (3) as an approachable, humanlike being, either by speculating on what he might look like ("He's the oldest person, so let's give him a long white beard"), personal realization, or with the guidance of sacred narrative and the insights of self-realized souls.

spiritual art in the west

Bhakti theology focuses on God the person, but acknowledges that there are three general stages of appreciating him. These correspond to the three approaches mentioned above. (1) We can know him as Brahman, an impersonal conception of God often thought of as a white light or the halo around his form; (2) as Paramatma, the Indweller, God as he exists in all things, localized, personal, dwelling in every being and in and between every atom; and (3) Bhagavan, the Supreme Person in all his glory and with his personality fully apparent – sometimes in his original form as Krishna, other times as Rama or Vishnu or one of his many other incarnations.

In looking at spiritual art, even in the West, it's helpful to understand these three aspects of the divine. Throughout its history, spiritual art (in any and all cultures) has

Wassily Kandinsky
Composition IV, 1911,
oil on canvas, 159.5 × 250.5 cm,
Kunstsammlung Nordrhein-Westfalen,
Düsseldorf, Germany

depicted the artist's vision of God in either his Brahman, Paramatma, or Bhagavan feature, even if the artists have not been consciously aware of it. Exactly which of these aspects a given artist focuses on will suggest his or her spiritual perceptions, the path he or she prefers to follow, his or her level of spiritual advancement, and the knowledge with which he or she approaches their art.

Interestingly, some of the most important Western artists of the modern period are aware of an indebtedness to Eastern cultures, particularly to the philosophical doctrines associated with India. For example, the Russian artist Wassily Kandinsky (1866–1944), famous for his abstract and "nonobjective" paintings, as well as his book *Concerning the Spiritual in Art* openly identified with the theosophical movement, which is based on Eastern thought. Kandinsky wrote that incorporating the "Asiatic discipline of meditation" could reinforce and facilitate artists in their work. His ideas on this subject were shared by Kupka, Mondrian, and Malevich, to name but a few of the famous painters fascinated by Eastern mysticism. These four began as Symbolist painters, but worked their way into abstract expressionism as their spiritual interests increased.

Others followed suit, Matisse and Klee the most notable. "We [artists] used to represent things visible on earth," Klee wrote in 1920, "things we either liked to look at or would have liked to see. Today we [attempt to] reveal the reality that is behind visible things, thus expressing the belief that the visible world is merely an isolated case in relation to the universe and that there are many other, latent realities ..."

Nonetheless, as each of these well-known artists rendered his own canvas with a distinctive brush, each gingerly dipped that brush into the unmistakable paint jar

Mark Rothko
Green, Red, on Orange, 1951,
oil on canvas, 236 × 150 cm

"The rivers are his veins, the trees his hairs, the air his breath, the sphere of outer space his eye pits ..."

The Vedas

of Eastern wisdom. And yet, influenced by theosophy, their canvases could only reflect the light of Brahman realization, a rudimentary aspect of the Absolute Truth. This is so because theosophy at best is only able to take its adherents to their stated goal: the impersonal Absolute. We may remember that Brahman is often envisioned as God's shining halo. Accordingly, Kandinsky writes that his artistic goal is to "proclaim the reign of the spirit ... to proclaim 'light from light, the flowing light of the Godhead, of the Holy Ghost.'" Attempts to illustrate this formless dimension of the Supreme were carried on by Rothko and Newman, among others, who sought to help their viewers understand the spiritual power of formlessness. These abstract expressionistic pointers to the divine embody the beginning of spiritual realization, which is necessarily partial, in the same way that the sunshine is only a partial representation of

the sun. Unfortunately, these painters were not exposed to bhakti theology, for here they would have discovered the Indweller (Paramatma), and Bhagavan, Krishna, the Supreme Person, along with his many incarnations and manifestations.

Modernity generally presupposes a break with tradition, and when artists become innovators in this way, conveying their spiritual perceptions without any longstanding connection to established religions, they can only invent their own symbols. Accordingly, there is no guarantee that those symbols will convey spiritual truth – or be spiritually moving to viewers. Rasa, on the other hand, is conveyed from a platform of abiding truth, not from imagination. It's also focused on relationship, not abstraction. Let it be known: It's hard, if not impossible, to reveal love through something that's abstract.

Indeed, there are artists who moved

beyond impersonal abstraction and attempted to portray God as he appears in nature – a rough parallel with Paramatma realization. As Edvard Munch wrote, "Art is the compulsion of man toward crystallization. Nature is the unique great realm upon which art feeds. Nature is not only what is visible to the eye – it also shows the inner images of the soul – the images on the backside of the eye ..." Philipp Otto Runge, from the Northern Romantic tradition, also expressed that "a sense of the mystical" could be found in all natural phenomena. Friedrich, Cole, Turner, and Church took these ideas further, almost visibly depicting Paramatma in their work – attempting to show, for example, the magnificence of God in the visible world, the unstoppable dictates of time, the relationship between the soul and the infinite, the overwhelming cosmos around us, the vast, unending spirituality of the sky. This suggestion of God's unlimited and pervasive existence in nature can be seen in Friedrich's *Monk by the Sea* as well as in other famous paintings in the West.

In actuality, the idea of Paramatma corresponds with the Western notion of panentheism, or God in nature, for his form is concealed to those of us who are not spiritually advanced. Because it's concealed, artists with little spiritual realization cannot depict it. When artists try to depict God as all-powerful and awe-inspiring nature, they seem to be aiming for what Western theology calls pantheism, God *as* nature. This latter perception of divinity is more congruous with "God as the universe," or the *virat-rupa,* spoken of in ancient Puranic texts: "The rivers are his veins, the trees his hairs, the air his breath, the sphere of outer space his eye pits ..." – details suitable for an in-depth meditation on God's greatness and a guide for a thoughtful artist.

Again, although artists in the West attempted to depict something akin to this

Statue of an Apsara,
early 12th century, sandstone,
Uttar Pradesh, India

divine aspect of nature, they could only do so in suggestive or representational ways: the bhakti texts that give elaborate specifics about the universal form and Brahman, Paramatma, and Bhagavan were until recently hidden away in archaic Sanskrit tomes.

Development of spiritual Art in India

Spiritual art in India developed in a very different way. From the beginning, Indian art has been associated with Vishnu and other personal manifestations of the supreme. An ancient narrative on the origins of art runs as follows: Vishnu, it is said, was sitting in deep meditation when several celestial dancing girls (*apsaras*) tried to distract him with their beauty. He indeed opened his eyes to them, as per their desire, but in awakening decided to help them overcome their vanity. To do this, he extracted the juice of a mango and, using it as paint, drew a beautiful woman with large, delicate eyes and incomparably gorgeous limbs. Her dimensions were enviable and her smile haunting. He named her Urvashi ("one who conquers the heart"). She was so attractive that the *apsaras* had to hide their faces in shame. Moreover, Vishnu breathed life into the painting, and, eventually, Urvashi became the feminine ideal – always young, ever charming, infinitely alluring. The attempt to capture Urvashi has been the goal of painters ever since. All beauty is said to emanate from her pores. Vishvakarma, architect of heaven, was soon taught the art and science of painting – of capturing this beauty – so he might transmit that knowledge to the people of the earth.

Tradition holds that in previous ages artistic representations were rarely needed. Art was solely for the glorification of Vishnu in the

Sri Yantra

From the beginning, Indian art has been associated with Vishnu and other personal manifestations of the Supreme.

form the worshiper most revered, and because he so often appeared in one form or another on earth, people had little need to paint images of him to remember him; he was personally present. As the final age – Kali-yuga, our current epoch – set in, Vishnu's appearances became rarer and people's memories of him short, so he made available to them an abundance of artistic techniques so they could depict him for the unfortunate souls who could not see him face to face.

The above history is expressed in the *Vishnu-dharmottara,* a section of the *Vishnu Purana* that deals with the arts. The text also instructs how to draw and paint God, humans, devas, and demons, how to make and use brushes and pigments, how to draw and paint light and shade, show proportion, and so on. The text elaborates on the importance of what we now call photorealism, and even outlines more abstract forms of art as well, such as the *yantra,*

a drawing of geometrical shapes that represents cosmic structures and alternate realities.

This sacred text also counsels artists to work within strictly defined parameters, urging them to adhere to specific rules in both their creations and their personal lives – art was considered holistic, not just a casual pastime or hobby, but engulfing every aspect of one's life. Artists were often also dancers – the two art forms were combined to help those who painted and danced familiarize themselves with bodily movements and gestures, which could then be moved from canvas to dance floor and back again.

Most importantly, all artists were encouraged to remain pure in thought and deed, as well as to practice spiritual disciplines, at least if they wanted the divinities they worshiped to reveal themselves in their art. To accomplish this, and to infuse their work with *rasa,* Indian artists have, for almost five thousand years,

Miniature of
Radha and Krishna

With his beauty, Krishna became the preeminent subject of Indian art.

traditionally followed the strictures of texts like the *Vishnu-dharmottara.* From the Vedic period to the modern day, artists have painted on palm leaves, walls, canvas, and paper, simply trying to evoke the divinity found in the pages of such sacred texts – and who is found in their heart of hearts as well.

In fact, the divine and his multifarious expansions and manifestations have graced artists' work from the beginning of recorded time. For example, Shiva, mystic yogi and powerful demigod, has been carved into cave walls for millennia. Such carvings cannot be dated – they flow back into inconceivable antiquity. And the same holds true for images of Indra, Ganesh, Hanuman, and other gods. None of them, however, has been painted or found dancing through illuminated manuscripts or posed in sculpture as much as one little blue cowherd boy, Krishna, who has always been depicted with unequalled frequency and enthusiasm. His

beautiful darkish skin, large lotus eyes, sweet flute adorning his lips, and peacock feather atop his raven-black hair, Krishna inevitably became the preeminent subject of Indian art.

Medieval manuscripts focused on scenes from the *Srimad-Bhagavatam* and *Gita Govinda* among other sacred texts. The love of Radha and Krishna, especially, was depicted in more paintings and sculptures than can be counted, the divinities revealing themselves in colors that showed the artists' personal realization and knowledge of sacred tradition.

A few examples: The Rajasthani School of painting, which was patronized by Rajput princes, produced an abundance of fine art. The Ragamala paintings stand out, with their fusion of musical rhythm and traditional symbolism – they focused on the love of Radha and Krishna, augmented by luscious depictions of beautiful seasonal changes, full-moon nights, and divine secret meetings between Krishna

Krishna Flirting with the Gopis, to Radha's Sorrow,
Kangra painting, ca. 1760

and the supremely spiritual, doe-eyed maidens of Vraja. Similar transcendent works would find their way from the hills of Punjab to the Deccan Plateau, a vast area in south-central India famous for its elaborate art. Nearly all of this art overflowed with bhakti-inspired themes rendered according to classical techniques outlined in scripture.

With the Mughal conquest in 1526, India's fine arts would know a radical change, both in terms of style and content. Nonetheless, depictions of Krishna, and even Rama, one of his chief incarnations, continued to be a central theme. Krishna's beauty and Rama's heroism were overwhelmingly alluring, so much so that even Muslim artists of the period could not resist painting their glorious pastimes, even though these divine figures did not speak to their theological interests. Much of this work was commissioned by Akbar, the famous emperor, who was himself sympathetic to the

ideals of bhakti, as has been documented by historians of the period.

Bundi, Jodhpur, Kishangarh, Basholi, Guler, Kangra, Tanjore – these are names little heard in the West. But for those familiar with India's artistic traditions, these names conjure images of distinct schools of bhakti art, including miniature painting, illuminated manuscripts, and folk art. The best of this work follows scriptural guidelines meticulously, and draws on centuries-old traditions. The goal, again, was to accurately depict the divine, not to indulge one's creative abilities or to show off individual talent.

"But what about self-expression?" one might ask. "Isn't that what art is *really* about?" In a sense, yes. But bhakti artists are always conscious of one persistent question: What can we express of a truly spiritual nature when we are bogged down by our material conditioning and unable to see transcendence? So part of

**His Divine Grace
A. C. Bhaktivedanta Swami Prabhupada**
Founder-Acharya of the International
Society for Krishna Consciousness

bhakti is humility, and artists inspired by devotion try to combine their own artistic ideas and experiences with those of self-realized masters and established texts in the hopes that they'll depict something that resembles spiritual truth. Otherwise, their work may hint at transcendence but will, in the end, produce nothing that's inspired with spiritual *rasa*.

Once an artist agrees to relinquish ego and submit to the spirit of the sages, he or she can dovetail their talent with God's energy, allowing a truly spiritual work to shine forth. It's then up to the viewers to perceive the spiritual content according to their own realization. Spiritual art is dynamic; it exists along a continuum of consciousness, and its spiritual potency is realized in progressive stages according to both the painter's ability to see into transcendence and the viewer's ability to perceive that subtle flow vibrating in the artwork. The same painting of Krishna that does nothing to move a neophyte in spiritual practice may elicit ecstasy in one who knows *rasa*.

Bhakti Art Comes West

Understanding the importance of transforming the consciousness both to create transcendental works of art and to appreciate them, the International Society for Krishna Consciousness (ISKCON), under the direction and guidance of His Divine Grace A. C. Bhaktivedanta Swami Prabhupada, the movement's founder and spiritual master, established a spiritual art department in 1966. Out of compassion for the world at large, Prabhupada was eager to publish his translations and explanations of ancient Vedic texts. He wanted these books beautified by transcendental paintings.

One of his first disciples, Jadurani Devi, had graduated from art school and was keen

Judy Koslofsky (Jadurani Devi Dasi)
Sri Pancha Tattva, 1966,
oil on canvas, 78 × 60 cm,
Museum of Sacred Art,
Durbuy, Belgium

"The greatest art is to understand Krishna ... to see the artistic hand of Krishna everywhere."

**His Divine Grace
A. C. Bhaktivedanta Swami Prabhupada**

to accommodate her spiritual master's vision. She joined in New York, where Prabhupada had established the first Hare Krishna temple in the West, and started painting soon after. To get her started with the iconography of bhakti, Prabhupada gave Jadurani a series of Indian prints to reproduce – one of Krishna and his eternal consort Radha in a bucolic environment with village friends and cows; one of Vishnu, Lord of the Universe; one of Sri Chaitanya, the combined manifestation of Radha and Krishna; and photos of saints in the bhakti line. It then became her task to render these on canvas, and eventually to prepare them for printing in Prabhupada's translations of the *Bhagavad-gita* and *Srimad-Bhagavatam (Bhagavata Purana)*.

At first it was slow going. Although not himself accomplished in the fine arts, Prabhupada personally trained his young artist disciple not only in the art of spiritual life, but in spiritual art. He taught her grid scaling methods and even suggested elements of design and layout. Drawing from texts like the *Vishnu-dharmottara* and the *Srimad-Bhagavatam,* he explained the dimensions of the divinities' forms along with the inner moods of their pastimes. Sometimes he even posed for her – imitating the man-lion Narasingha's ferocity, or, at other times, raising his hands gracefully to his lips as if playing a flute, like Krishna. Most of all, he instructed her in the minutiae of bhakti philosophy and aesthetics – including the skin color, mounts, symbols, and dress of divine personalities, and the settings in which they would normally appear.

"The greatest art," he explained, "is to understand Krishna. If we actually want to be artists, we should try to understand – or try to be intimately associated with – the greatest artist, Krishna.... That is Krishna consciousness – to see the artistic hand of Krishna everywhere."

By 1967 Prabhupada had dubbed Jadurani

Puskar Dasa showing newer works from
the art department to Prabhupada,
New York, ca. 1972.

his "art directress," for now other artists had
joined his fledgling movement and he wanted
her to train them as he had trained her. That
same year, Govinda Dasi, after graduating from
the University of Texas as an art major, joined
Prabhupada in San Francisco. Separated from
Jadurani Devi by more than three thousand
miles, Prabhupada gave Govinda Dasi the same
attention and instruction he had given his New
York artist. Meanwhile, Jadurani was training a
flood of new artists in New York.

In the late '60s the art department moved
to Boston, where ISKCON Press (pre-cursor to
the Bhaktivedanta Book Trust, or BBT) made
its long-awaited appearance. Painters like
Muralidhara, Baradraj, and Pariksit teamed up
with Jadurani to create ISKCON masterpieces –
a number of which appear in this book.

In the '70s ISKCON Press moved to
Brooklyn, and more artists came forward.
Eventually, the art department became so

large that it moved to Los Angeles, where the
BBT had set up its central headquarters. There,
a new generation of artists – Puskar, Dhriti,
Ramadasa Abhirama Dasa, Drigha, and others – brought bhakti painting to newer heights.
This dynamic progression is still alive and ac-
tive today. With bhakti now an international
movement, bhakti-inspired artists are painting
in Eastern Europe, England, Australia, Africa,
and India, and their work is creating a unique
fusion of East and West, modern and ancient –
using contemporary methods and materials
to depict the eternal truth of the soul and the
spirit of all spirits, Krishna himself.

Avatar Art: Neo-vedic paintings celebrating Life

The book you now hold in your hands is
a sampling of unique spirituality and ancient
heritage.

Ramadasa Abhirama Dasa (standing),
Muralidhara Dasa (back, seated),
and Pariksit Dasa.

It should be noted that while the images in this book are commonly associated with India, bhakti, devotion to God, is a universal expression, present in all abiding spiritual paths. Krishna is the same God who is revered in the Abrahamic religions, even though he has his own unique appearance in Indian-based bhakti theology. Demigods like Brahma, Shiva, Ganesh, and Hanuman are like the many angels or divine helpers who assist in God's mission in all cultures.

Also note that the majority of artists whose work appears in this volume are not Indian but are from North America and Europe. This is a testament to the power of the bhakti tradition – it transcends culture and creed and speaks to the hearts of people the world over.

Because the majority of these painters were trained in Western art schools, their art marries Indian imagery with traditionally European painting styles. Most of this art will remind the viewer of a neo-Renaissance style, with elements of the pre-Raphaelites, the Orientalists, and of Victorian art. The discerning art critic can locate influences from Reubens, Bouguereau, Leighton, Fragonard, David, Ingres, Caravaggio, and many others, and from the Russian schools, Repin, Kramskoy, Shishkin, Vasnetsov, and Kuindji. In appearance, the work generally looks classical or neoclassical, using techniques developed in the West in the early nineteenth century. The only difference is in the mood and, of course, the subject matter. If one considers these influences, much of this art, at least stylistically, becomes understandable.

Style aside, bhakti art is meant to give pleasure to the eye and nourishment to the soul. So please enjoy the art simply and directly, while tasting the spiritual profundity that lies at its core.

Avatars, Devas, sages, and Demons

Whenever we see the descent of the divine as avatar, we are witnessing a meeting of two worlds, the spiritual and the mundane. An avatar doesn't order humans about from on high or absent himself from their small doings, but he steps onto the earth to play, sometimes as a fantastical being and sometimes as a being more human than we are ourselves – and always for a purpose.

This play of the divine begins with creation. It then invigorates the exertions of the devas – bringers of light and cosmic order – and the power-hungry demons; of the sages, distributors of the sacred to humans, and the heroes of every description who populate all the cosmic and everyday dramas of a universe at work.

It's an avatar who dances the worlds into destruction, too, and who then rests on a watery bed in mystic slumber until he's ready to play again.

Marek Buchwald (Baradraj Dasa)
Vishnu on Shesha, 1981,
oil on canvas, 40 × 28 cm

Keshava

Oil on canvas, 210 × 136 cm

Keshava, "He with the beautiful hair," is an avatar of **Krishna,** and here we see him standing in the luminous, infinite waters of creation, from which the worlds will emerge. He is the color of a rain-washed sky, and he rises out of the water with the four attributes that signify the universal protector – the conch, lotus, mace, and chakra.

Keshava is often depicted lying on a thousand-headed snake named Shesha, "Timeless," and even here we see Shesha's hoods painted stylistically, almost blossoming over Keshava's head. One of his coils seems to serve as an armrest just below the hand holding the lotus.

Keshava's conch is called Panchajanya, and it is the source of the five great elements (earth, water, fire, air, and ether, or space). The conch is said to sound the primeval vibration from which creation develops.

His chakra, Sudarshana, has six spokes, symbolizing his control over humankind's six evil inclinations: lust, anger, greed, illusion, envy, and bewilderment. The chakra is a fearful weapon, and is used for lopping off the heads of demons.

The lotus, symbol of purity, represents the unfolding of creation and indicates the presence of **Lakshmi,** Keshava's eternal feminine counterpart.

And the mace, Kaumodaki, represents the elemental force from which all physical and mental powers derive, as well as God's ultimate and unsurpassable strength.

Keshava also means "one who killed Keshi," a demon who appeared near the beginning of creation. Keshava, as an avatar of Krishna, is unlimited, yet Keshi thought him weaker than himself and tried to kill him in a crushing embrace. How is it possible to encircle the unlimited with limited arms?

> **He is the color of a rain-washed sky, and he rises out of the water with the four attributes that signify the universal protector.**

Brahma, Vishnu, Shiva

Oil on canvas, 48 × 75 cm

Here we see the three deities responsible for universal creation, maintenance, and destruction, Brahma (left), Vishnu (center), and Shiva (right), depicted in poses typical of each. Vishnu, being the Supreme Personality of Godhead, is the root of what many call the "Hindu trinity," and as such he accepts the more difficult role of maintaining the creation. Being the root, Vishnu also provides the blueprint for creation, which he passes on to four-headed Brahma, seen here holding the scrolled Vedas. Brahma is vastly intelligent – the Vedas say that even his body is made of pure intelligence – and he takes Vishnu's blueprint and creates a self-sustaining world.

But creation is only one-third of the cosmic order. In the upper left-hand corner of the painting we see it beginning. Planets spin into being above the bare rock of the landscape. After the creation is underway, Brahma fathers Shiva and assigns him the role of destroyer. Shiva is often depicted, as here, performing his *tandava-nritya,* or dance of devastation, intended to break the material elements into their constituent parts until all forms as we know them dissolve. The same worlds Brahma is creating on the left side of the painting explode over the dancing Shiva's head on the right. Volcanoes erupt and black fissures run through the rock. Holding the fire of destruction in one hand and his *damaru* drum in another, Shiva dances the worlds into annihilation.

Brahma and Shiva flank Vishnu, who literally steals the spotlight – both creation and destruction take place in the dark, but the period between them is filled with light. Vishnu, eyes half-closed in yogic trance, is maintaining and supporting what has been created on his order. His attributes of both protection and blessing are prominent.

The macrocosmic function of each of these three persons is symbolically reflected in each living being: Brahma is not only the creator, but the creative function; Vishnu maintains or preserves the outer world, but he is also the indwelling soul, preserving life; and Shiva not only destroys the cosmos at the appropriate time in the cycle of ages, but serves as the catalyst for inner transformation.

Shiva is often depicted, as here, performing his tandava-nritya, or dance of devastation.

Paramatma, "the Indweller"

Oil on canvas, 75 × 57 cm

"The Indweller" is the Soul of our soul and the heart of every atom. He is **Krishna** as Supersoul, the ecstatic and almighty life and soul of the living being. As our soul is dear to us, so the Soul of our soul is even dearer. The Indweller is the still, small voice of conscience, the witness, the permitter, and the friend who never abandons. He accompanies all living beings as they inhabit one body after another up and down through the species.

The *Upanishads* describe the soul and Supersoul as two birds sitting on the branch of a tree. The individual soul tastes the bitter and sweet fruits, while the Supersoul simply watches and sanctions. The tree symbolizes the mundane world, and the fruits are the soul's endless material desires and their karmic results. The Supersoul is the impartial witness and support of each being's activities and the dispenser of karma. He tastes neither mundane enjoyment nor suffering, but waits with a heart full of spiritual joy for the living beings to end their enchantment with the world of matter and turn to him in search of a truer happiness.

The artist has based his painting on a description of the Indweller given for meditation in the *Srimad-Bhagavatam:* "His eyes spread like the petals of a lotus, and his garments, yellow like the saffron of a kadamba flower, are bedecked with valuable jewels. His ornaments are all made of gold set with jewels, and he wears a glowing headdress and earrings. His lotus feet are placed over the whorls of the lotuslike hearts of great mystics. He is garlanded with fresh flowers and well decorated with an ornamental wreath about his waist. His leglets, his bangles, his oiled blackish hair, curling with a bluish tint, and his beautiful smiling face are all very pleasing."

The Supersoul sits side by side with the individual soul, the *Upanishads* tell us, and meditation means to go in search of him. The soul is like the gold pendant on the necklace of self, and the Indweller the brilliant jewel set in the gold. If a yogi sees the necklace but not the jewel, his or her meditation is not yet complete.

The Indweller accompanies all living beings as they inhabit one body after another up and down through the species.

Lakshmi, the Divine Feminine

Oil on canvas, 26 × 20 cm

Lakshmi, Sri, is the divine feminine energy. **Vishnu** is God, the supreme potent, and Lakshmi is shakti, his dynamic energy. The potent is known through its potency just as a perfume is recognized by its fragrance. If the potency is separated from the potent, the potent no longer has meaning. What is fire without heat? Lakshmi and Vishnu are eternally distinct personalities, but they are ever nondifferent and inseparable.

As Vishnu is the primordial God, so Lakshmi is the primordial goddess, mother of the created universe and fountainhead of all other goddesses. She personifies love, opulence, and compassion. Always in Vishnu's service, she stands as mediator between God and humankind. While Vishnu can be stern and demanding, Lakshmi is forgiving and tolerant. If a devotee tries to supplicate Vishnu, he or she may more readily know success by approaching him through his softer side, Lakshmi, his consort.

Whenever Vishnu descends as an avatar, Lakshmi descends with him. When he comes as **Rama,** she comes as Sita; when he appears as **Krishna,** she is his queen, **Rukmini.** Lakshmi is never without Vishnu. The *Puranas* are full of stories of persons who tried to separate them and were vanquished. The most famous of these is the *Ramayana,* where Ravana stole Sita from Rama and was ruined.

Lakshmi is venerated as the goddess of fortune and beauty. The *Puranas* describe her as hauntingly beautiful, with large, lotuslike eyes and a golden complexion. The *Lakshmi-tantra* says that her smile is subtle and her red lips gemlike. Her teeth resemble pearls and her forehead a half moon. Her glance embodies her spirit of devotion to Vishnu.

Here she has been painted in moody colors, her demeanor meditative. The bindi over her third eye glows on her forehead. The dot signifies female energy, and its red color is symbolic of the seeing power that comes with the rising of the sun. Bindis protect the feminine energy from dissipation and ward off evil influences for both the wearer and the object of her devotion.

Lakshmi personifies love, opulence, and compassion.

Narada, "wisdom-giver"

Oil on canvas, 60 × 45 cm

Narada is the "wisdom-giver," the "one who gives Narayana," and a mind-born son of **Brahma.** He is an accomplished yogi and sage, and he travels between the spiritual and material worlds on subtle pathways through outer space.

Narada is an avatar of bhakti yoga – not a descent of **Krishna,** but a soul empowered by Krishna to teach the principles of devotion wherever he goes. Many of his disciples are as famous as he is – the great "compiler" **Vyasa, Prahlad,** son of the demon **Hiranya-kashipu,** King **Dhruva,** and Valmiki, author of the *Ramayana* – and some almost unknown, such as the hunter Mrigari, who under Narada's tutelage renounced violence for compassion.

Vishnu presented Narada with a veena in recognition of Narada's devotion to him, and Narada is rarely depicted without it. For his song, Narada claimed the seven singing meters of the musical scale crafted by Brahma during the creation and formed them into kirtan to glorify Krishna and his avatars. Narada has been associated with devotional music ever since.

The veena is an ancient instrument. Both excavations and ancient Vedic texts reveal that India had a developed musical culture, and that veenas were used even during what is known as the Indus Valley civilization. In this painting the artist has taken liberties with Narada's veena and painted him with a relatively modernized instrument, now called the *saraswati* veena, recognizable by its two resonators. Note the ornamentation at both ends of the fingerboard, especially the swan's head at the top, symbolic of Saraswati, goddess of learning and the arts.

For his song, Narada claimed the seven singing meters of the musical scale crafted during the creation and formed them into kirtan to glorify Krishna and his avatars.

Pariksit and the snake-Bird

Oil on canvas, 54 × 40 cm

The *Srimad-Bhagavatam's* central narrative begins with the cursing of Pariksit, last of the noble Vedic kings. Some five thousand years ago, Pariksit was wandering through a forest when he came to the hermitage of the sage Shamik, who was rapt in meditation. Entering the sage's dwelling, Pariksit expected to be honored – or at least offered the simple courtesies one would extend any weary traveler. But the sage continued his meditation, eyes closed.

His throat parched and his mood darkening, and seeing a dead snake lying nearby, Pariksit lifted the snake with his bow and draped it around the sage's neck. The sage did not stir. Then Pariksit returned to his palace.

When the sage's son saw the insult offered his father, he cursed Pariksit: "Seven days from today a snake-bird will appear and take your life."

On the seventh day – the scene depicted here – we find Pariksit being burned alive by the snake-bird Takshaka. Note the artist's depiction of leathery, taloned wings as the snake-bird reaches up to bite the king. Its dragonlike appearance is ominous, but the artist has situated King Pariksit atop the kind of stone structure frequently seen at riverside bathing places around India, elevating him to a commanding position in the composition and stressing his importance and power.

Six days before this scene, the king had inquired about the duty of a man about to die. He had been advised to hear the *Srimad-Bhagavatam* from a self-realized soul, and **Shukadeva,** best of all such souls, had graciously served this function.

But on the seventh day, **Kashyapa,** a well-known mystic, was enlisted to counteract the curse. Takshaka, however, bribed Kashyapa with treasure. Here we see the sage making off with his pot of gold. Takshaka was magically able to assume any form. He appeared as a brahmin so he could approach the king, surrounded as he was by an assembly of sages. When Takshaka was close enough, he reverted to his original hideous form and bit the king.

By the time he died, we're told, Pariksit had achieved both fearlessness and a vision of God. Here, Pariksit looks transcendent as his body is consumed by flames. One would expect the assembled sages to recoil in fear at the sight of Takshaka, but they rush to Pariksit's aid. The sages' hearts too had been liberated from the fear of death by Shukadeva's teachings. Here we see them wanting to protect the king from harm, raising their staffs as if to beat Takshaka back.

Pariksit meets кali

Oil on canvas, 113 × 170 cm

King Pariksit was born just as the world changed seasons from the third age to the fourth, Kali-yuga, the winter of an ever-cycling set of four ages. Pariksit inherited the throne from the high-minded Pandavas and was in his own right a powerful advocate of dharma. He was also a great devotee of **Krishna,** who advented not long before his birth to establish the religion of bhakti.

After Pariksit became king, he saw signs of the onset of the world's winter. Kali-yuga, he knew, is characterized by hypocrisy, bitter quarrels, uncontrolled lusts, pollution, and war. Arming himself and mounting his chariot, he set out to drive the signs of the age from his kingdom.

Soon he came on the personification of Kali-yuga – a lowborn demon dressed as a king, viciously beating a bull and cow with a club and cutting off the bull's legs.

The bull represents dharma, or spiritual culture, and its four legs represent truthfulness, cleanliness, austerity, and mercy. With the bull's legs gone, these virtuous qualities leave the world as well.

Pariksit arrested the demon in king's clothing, but not before three of the bull's legs had been cut off. Only the leg representing truthfulness remained. Kali, who flourishes by deceit, is still trying to destroy this last leg.

The artist has chosen to depict the advent of Kali-yuga with a montage. In the upper left corner of the painting we see the hallmarks of Kali's rule: images of animal slaughter, intoxication, sexual promiscuity, and gambling. Although a purple-clad Kali is kneeling in surrender at the sight of Pariksit's upraised sword, the tree of his influence, framed by a gathering storm, arches over both Kali and the king. Kali's cloak merges with the cow's blood at the root of the tree, symbolizing his part in the age's violence.

Pariksit's attempt to protect dharmic principles was for everyone's good, because truthfulness, cleanliness, austerity, and mercy have value in every culture. Unfortunately, we tend to be blind to the fact that these virtues are directly countered by the vices of gambling, promiscuous sex, intoxication, and meat-eating. Pariksit was unable to overcome the force of the age, and these degrading activities continue to proliferate.

Yet the age has one advantage. The *Upanishads* tell us that should the holy name of Krishna enter the mind but once, it will counteract the ugly unhappiness of materialism and instill dharma and devotion in the heart.

shukadeva

Oil on canvas, 109 × 147 cm

Shukadeva is famous for speaking the *Srimad-Bhagavatam* to **Pariksit,** who had been cursed to die in seven days. Shukadeva, son of **Vyasa,** the original compiler of the Vedas, was preeminently qualified to share the essence of the *Purana's* wisdom with Pariksit. *Shuka* means "parrot," and like a parrot, Shukadeva melodiously repeated the teachings that had been handed down like a ripe mango plucked from a tree by **Vishnu** to creator **Brahma** to **Narada** to Shuka's great father Vyasa, and finally to himself.

Liberated from birth, Shukadeva spent his time wandering about in a divinely intoxicated state, a naked mendicant absorbed in the unity behind creation and Krishna's pastimes with his many devotees. No one recognized his exalted status until he arrived at the riverbank to speak; a true sage is recognized by what he says.

This painting details Shukadeva's first meeting with Pariksit. Pariksit, facing imminent death, had come to the bank of the **Ganges** River to ask the sages there a question: "Please tell me the duty of those about to die." The sages were unable to give a conclusive reply. Shukadeva enters the scene just at this moment.

The artist has painted the sages standing or sitting to the side, shadowed by trees and occupying two thirds of the canvas. The kneeling young king, dressed simply as befits a spiritual aspirant, and a naked Shukadeva take up the other third of the canvas, bathed in light and framed by a holy mountain, symbolic of Vedic wisdom.

Notice the banyan tree at the center of the painting, with its branches growing downward and its roots up. The banyan is a frequent symbol in Indian art, reminding the viewer that the material world is a reflection of the spiritual. The yogis under it sit in rigid asceticism yet remain in the dark. Shukadeva, however, bends softly, reaching down to the king with compassion. While the banyan tree divides the king and his guide from the yogis, the sky arches over everyone, leading one to imagine that even those in the dark can achieve enlightenment.

It's interesting to note that the artist has not placed Pariksit and Shukadeva in the foreground of the painting. Pariksit's question is large and its answer of vital import to all of us (who among us will not die?). Still, we are tiny members of a vastly greater world.

Vyasa, "the compiler"

Oil on canvas, 52 × 40 cm

Sage Vyasa, the great seer and avatar of **Krishna,** looked into the future and saw the shadow of the Age of Kali falling over the earth. During this age, Vyasa knew, people are short-lived, distracted, and have meager education, and he realized that this meant people would not be able to memorize the sacred Veda, as was traditional. So he compiled the Veda, then divided it into three, and added any necessary explanations. Next, he wrote supplementary treatises and a fourth Veda, and compiled many of the *Puranas,* histories, and the epic, *Mahabharata.*

But when he was finished, Vyasa was surprised to feel despondent. He had wanted his work to serve as a guide through the darkness of Kali-yuga, but he realized he had buried the essence of his message – and the remedy to the ills of the age – in a flood of unqualified information.

As he despaired, his guru **Narada** arrived. Narada listened to Vyasa's problem and said, "To see the self means to see God also. To teach self-realization without teaching how to find God doesn't help anyone. You have actually taught people how to use religion to fulfill their material desires, and this will only bind them to the painful wheel of action and reaction. You have descended to earth for others' well-being. Please therefore correct your mistake by writing another work that vividly describes the transcendental pastimes of the Supreme Person, Sri Krishna, so that people will find their eternal relationship with him." After saying this, Narada left.

The artist has painted the scene just after Narada's departure. Vyasa, sitting in his ashram at Samyaprash, above modern-day Haridwar, then closed his eyes in meditation and linked his mind with God in bhakti yoga. Looking through the golden glowing veil of Brahman, he saw the face of the Original Person. Standing behind this Original Person were God's energies, which are never separated from him, as moonlight is never separated from the moon. He then understood that although the living beings are by nature spiritual, they think themselves products of the material energy, and so they suffer.

Here we see Vyasa looking out, his eyes alight with the weight of his spiritual maturity. His stylus is poised as he records his vision. This record became what sages later called "the ripened fruit of the Vedic tree of knowledge," the *Bhagavata Purana,* or *Srimad-Bhagavatam.*

41

Matsya, the Fish Avatar

Oil on canvas, 120 × 85 cm

The *Puranas* say that **Vishnu** incarnates in each species of life to show mercy democratically. Vishnu's fish avatar appeared near the end of the last millennium, when it was close to the time for the cyclical universal annihilation.

Satyavrata, "devoted to truth," was a great king and sage. Just before Matsya appeared to him, he had spent some days fasting only on water and in the mornings going to a nearby river to make simple offerings of palmfuls of water to Vishnu.

One day, he was surprised to see he had scooped up a small fish in his hand. Seeing the struggling creature, he threw it back into the river, saying, "Swim, little fish. Go home."

But mysteriously, the fish spoke back: "Why do you throw me back into the water? Don't you know that there are other fish here who might eat me? Please protect me." Unaware of the tiny fish's divinity but realizing the fish's specialness, the kind Satyavrata placed him in a small jug and brought him home.

The mystical fish grew overnight, and so he asked Satyavrata to find a larger water pot in which he could live. But every time the king found a new pot for him, the fish outgrew it. The fish then asked to be placed back in the river. When he expanded beyond the river's banks, the king moved him to the ocean.

But the fish continued to grow. When he was several miles longer than the breadth of the ocean, the king finally asked, "Who are you? You are bewildering me." At that time Vishnu revealed both his identity and his plan.

From this point on, the story appears too similar to that of the biblical Noah and other flood narratives to be coincidental. The divine Matsya told Satyavrata he would save him from the worldwide deluge that was soon to follow, and he instructed him to board a ship he would send, bringing with him the sages, animals, and plants. Satyavrata should also tie the ship to Matsya's "horn."

When the ocean began to rise, a boat appeared, and Satyavrata followed Matsya's instructions. By this time Matsya had grown to a tremendous size, and he easily navigated the massive floodwaters, towing the boat behind him until the danger had subsided.

Mysteriously, the fish spoke back: "Why do you throw me back into the water?"

KEVIN YEE (RAMADASA ABHIRAMA DASA)
MIRIAM BRIKS (DHRITI DEVI DASI)

vamana, the Dwarf Avatar

Oil on canvas, 26 × 20 cm

The story of **Vishnu's** three strides as the dwarf-avatar Vamana is ancient. King Bali, born in the line of demons but grandson of the great devotee **Prahlad,** was not an evil king, yet he was obsessed with wealth and his reputation as the most charitable. The *Puranas* tell us he became so powerful that he was able to control the three worlds. This offset the universe's symmetry, so to restore balance Vishnu appeared in the form of a dwarf brahmin.

Bali knew that those who give richly to brahmins are well rewarded so, when Vamana approached him as he was concluding a Vedic sacrifice with the customary offering of charity, he was prepared to offer him anything.

But Vamana's request was so unassuming that Bali was taken aback. Vamana said, "O generous King, all I ask is a strip of land as large as I can cover in three of my footsteps." Bali looked at the small brahmin's feet. The request was ludicrous, even naive. To look out for the young brahmin's interests, Bali insisted Vamana accept a plot at least big enough for a cottage. Vamana declined, then spoke of the danger of wanting more than one needs. Bali acquiesced and granted the small piece of land.

As soon as the king agreed, however, Vamana began to grow. Within minutes the dwarf was a giant. Taking his first step, he covered the world. Growing still larger, his second step reached to the ends of the heavens. Bali recognized his Lord Vishnu in this brahmin, so he said, "You have covered all of existence in two steps. Please place your third step on my head." Vamana was pleased with Bali's humility and blessed him.

The sacrificial arena is shown on the shadowy lower left periphery of the painting. Bali is almost in the center of the canvas, his hands lifted in prayer. Bali must have realized, as Vamana grew to enormous proportions, that he was about to plunge from king of the universe to an unknown fate. Still, he surrenders to Vishnu's desire.

To capture the spirit of the relationship between Vamana and Bali, the artist has muted the lines of both their bodies, softening even the figures shielding themselves in fear, allowing the viewer to glimpse the underlying love being exchanged between God and his devotee.

Vamana wears a *kiritamukut,* or "highest of crowns," on his head, symbolizing his infallible ability to follow through on his word. He means to bless Bali with his highest mercy; his crown indicates he has the power to do so.

The Innocent Kumaras

Oil on canvas, 35 × 25 cm

The sage-avatars Sanaka, Sanatana, Sananda, and Sanat-Kumara are mind-born sons of **Brahma.** They were born early in the creation, and Brahma, the universal engineer and first progenitor, asked them to father children to help populate the universe. But they chose to remain as children; they wanted to remain concentrated on the oneness of **Vishnu** and his energies without the troublesome distractions that come with physical maturity.

This painting shows the Kumaras as they have just traveled to the spiritual world, abode of Narayana (Vishnu). Although as children the Kumaras were accustomed to passing through any gate unhindered, the gatekeepers of the spiritual world barred the Kumaras' entrance because the boys had not realized anything beyond the truth that God pervades everything. If they were to enter, how would they understand the unlimitedly beautiful Narayana or his relationships with his pure devotees?

The Kumaras cursed the gatekeepers – an act they later regretted – and the scene in this painting shows Narayana suddenly arriving on the scene. Notice that he is barefoot – he came quickly to mediate the conflict between his devoted gatekeepers and the Kumaras and didn't take the time to put on his shoes.

This is the Kumaras' first meeting with Narayana. Previously they had thought him only an energy, but in his presence this conception faded like a dream. His beauty was stunning. His face, framed by raven hair, reminded them of the inner whorl of a blue lotus, and his shower of loving glances made them reel in ecstasy. They gazed at his beautiful golden garment falling in graceful pleats, his silky lilac shawl, his sweet-smelling garland swaying in the breeze, his ruby toenails. The fragrance of the holy tulasi leaves on his feet thrilled their senses. This was the Narayana who would now become their deepest meditation.

The artist has shown the Kumaras as innocents, gathering around Narayana as children gather around a father who has been too long absent. Narayana bends over them in a universally parental pose, and one of the Kumaras leans upward to meet his affectionate gaze. We feel that Narayana is about to embrace them, yet here his arms remain open, bearing his characteristic symbols of protection, purity, eternality, and creative power.

The fragrance of the holy tulasi leaves on his feet thrilled their senses.

Kapila, son of Devahuti

Oil on canvas, 54 × 45 cm

Sage **Kardama** once meditated for ten thousand years. As a result of his austerities he was rewarded with a vision of **Vishnu.** Offering many prayers before his Lord, Kardama begged him for a wife, someone of like mind who could appreciate and participate in his spiritual endeavors. He wanted to conceive a child who would be an avatar of Vishnu, someone with the power to teach people the ultimate path to self-realization.

Vishnu suggested Kardama marry **Devahuti.** The couple named their son Kapila. After fathering Kapila, Kardama considered his life's mission complete. He renounced the world and returned to his meditation in the forest.

Kapila was particularly empowered to spread the path of *sankhya yoga* – a blend of mysticism, philosophical analysis, and bhakti.

Now alone with her divine son, Devahuti said to Kapila, "You are the ax to cut the tree of material existence. Please explain to me the relationship between man and woman, spirit and matter."

Kapila began with a description of creation, and then analyzed the material elements and their interactions. He taught his mother how to recognize her own soul and the soul in all other beings, to recognize God and any true spiritual seeker.

When Kapila completed his instructions, he too left home, and here we see him wandering in the wilderness. Above him, the Gandharvas, the musicians of the devas, shower flowers and blow trumpets in praise. Yogis have broken their solitary meditation and gathered on the mountaintop to offer him respect as he passes.

Kapila looks directly at the viewer, but his look is subdued; it is the look of one who is at peace with himself. The artist has portrayed his inner harmony by giving him a god's physique – he bears no signs of the withering that usually marks those who practice asceticism – and a gentler than expected scale between the mighty Himalayan mountains and the sage. Kapila expresses neither fear nor loneliness, but instead we feel a compassionate invitation to join him in his turning from the world of the body to the life of the spirit.

"Please explain to me the relationship between man and woman, spirit and matter."

sagara's sons immolated

Oil on canvas, 51 × 38 cm

King Sagara, born in the Age of Yajña (sacrifice) and famous for having fathered sixty thousand sons, decided to perform a horse sacrifice to gain favor with **Vishnu.** Such sacrifices gave immense power. **Indra,** lord of the celestial spheres, worried that Sagara wanted to extend his rulership of earth to the throne of the heavens, so he stole the horse. The horse was not easily replaced; sacrificial animals needed specific characteristics before they could be offered. It might take years of breeding to get another suitable horse.

So King Sagara ordered his sixty thousand sons to search for the missing animal. The boys finally found the creature at the ashram of **Kapila,** the sage-avatar of Vishnu. "Here is the man who has stolen the horse," they shouted. "Look! He's sitting with his eyes closed, pretending to meditate. Kill him!" But as they raised their weapons, their disrespect for the great saint flared up as fire in their bodies, and they were burned to ashes.

When his sons failed to return, King Sagara sent his grandson, Amsuman, to search for both the horse and the lost men. Eventually Amsuman traced them to where Kapila sat, now framed by Amsuman's uncles' remains.

The sacrificial horse grazed nearby. When Amsuman saw Kapila, he folded his hands in respect and said: "O **Indweller** of all beings, simply by seeing you, I have become free of the greed that causes karmic bondage."

Hearing these pleasing words, Kapila replied, "Here is the animal sought by your grandfather for his sacrifice. Please take it. As for your uncles, their bodies have been burned to ashes and their souls trapped by their offense. Only **Ganges** water can purify them and free their souls."

In this painting, Amsuman sits before Kapila and realizes the task he is being asked to perform. The Ganges is a celestial river; if he is to rescue the souls of his uncles from hell, he must somehow find a way to draw the Ganges to earth. He kneels with folded hands before Kapila, seeking his way, even as the dark clouds hanging over the mountains in the background offer a hint: he is to take up a life of penance and renunciation. The sunburst in the center of the painting, spanning the sky between the richly dressed Amsuman and the simply dressed but self-satisfied yogi, reflects the enlightenment Amsuman can attain if he chooses to follow Kapila's path.

JUDY KOSLOFSKY (JADURANI DEVI DASI) 1974

Maitreya instructs vidura

Oil on canvas, 69 × 52 cm

Vidura, "the wise one," seen here on the left, is described in the *Mahabharata* as the Pandavas' chief advisor and protector after their father died. The Pandavas were in frequent danger from their scheming cousin Duryodhana, who succeeded in usurping their throne when they came of age.

Once, while trying to argue the Pandavas' case before **Dhritarastra,** Duryodhana's father and his own elder brother, Vidura was insulted and evicted from the palace. Accepting this turn of events as God's will, Vidura decided to go on pilgrimage to all the holy places. He traveled alone, his mind absorbed in devotion to Krishna, to places where "the air and water were pure and the forms of **Vishnu** decorated the temples."

At last he reached the source of the **Ganges** at Haridwar. There, he met sage Maitreya and accepted him as his teacher.

Here, Vidura and Maitreya sit on an islet in a gently flowing stream. Vidura sits with his hands folded in obeisance, his head turned to the side as if to better catch Maitreya's words. We imagine the water flowing down from the solidity of the rocks and circling the islet to represent the stream of sweet words flowing from Maitreya to Vidura. This is a romantic scene, depicting the dream of all seekers of the truth to wander through the wilds, their hearts transfigured by beauty, and to suddenly find themselves face to face with an old and self-realized master who can answer all their questions. Maitreya means "friend", and here we see him reaching both hands out, palms open. He is simply giving, neither expecting nor needing anything in return.

The artist could have expanded the painting out into the open air to give us a sense of the immensity of the topics the two were discussing, but instead she chose to bound student and teacher by rocks, water, and trees. The background is verdant but mostly dark. It does not distract the eye from the complete world of the islet. This is an extremely personal encounter, and we, like the flowers in the foreground of the painting, lean in to receive Maitreya's gift of knowledge.

**Vidura asks Maitreya:
"Please give us directions
on how one should live
for real happiness."**

Narasingha, the "Man-Lion"

Oil on canvas, 120 × 100 cm

Narasingha, avatar of **Vishnu** and carrying his attributes, is half-man, half-lion. He is the ferocious avatar, and his sharp teeth, unsheathed claws, and roar for the blood of the demon-king **Hiranya-kashipu** distinguish him from Vishnu's other forms.

Narasingha fulfills the *Bhagavad-gita's* statement that Vishnu descends to protect his devotees and kill those who torture them. He is aggressively protective, but otherwise, like other avatars, he is gentle and benevolent.

Narasingha's softer feature is beautifully depicted here by Janmanalaya Dasa, who has painted Narasingha with a cosmic palette spanning from indigos to sunny oranges and golden yellows to indicate that Narasingha is an avatar for all times and all places in the universe. Spiritual aspirants pray to him to kill their inner demons, just as he destroyed the power-mad Hiranya-kashipu. Narasingha's chakra glitters as it spins on his finger, hinting at his power to keep us safe.

A seven-headed Shesha rises behind Narasingha's helmeted head. Shesha's coiling and uncoiling control the constant ebb and flow of favorable and unfavorable circumstances, as he is controlled by the dominant Narasingha.

Narasingha's chakra glitters as it spins on his finger, hinting at his power to keep his devotees safe.

Hiranya-kashipu

Oil on canvas, 148 × 109 cm

Devas, sages, and demons practice asceticism to gain invincibility, unusual longevity, or magic. Hiranya-kashipu, king of the demons, and his twin brother, Hiranyaksha, practiced severe austerities to attain immortality. Thinking himself successful, Hiranyaksha had gone off in search of worthy opponents, been directed to **Vishnu**, and been killed.

Hearing the news, Hiranya-kashipu set out to avenge his brother. When he couldn't find Vishnu, however, he assumed Vishnu was hiding in fear of him. He then threw the devas out of the heavens and declared himself supreme in Vishnu's place.

Actually, when he had first asked **Brahma** for immortality, Brahma had told him it wasn't in his power to grant this. Hiranya-kashipu then modified his request in such a way that he was convinced he had tricked Brahma. He asked that he not be killed indoors or outdoors, on the ground or in the air, by day or by night, by man or by beast, or by any weapon known to man. Since this covered all the ways Hiranya-kashipu could think of that someone could be killed, he felt indestructible.

But his youngest son **Prahlad** was a problem. Prahlad was devoted to Hiranya-kashipu's enemy, Vishnu. Enraged by this betrayal, Hiranya-kashipu ordered the boy killed. Vishnu again and again rescued the boy.

Furious, the demon-king demanded of his five-year-old son, "Show me your Vishnu!"

Prahlad replied, "Vishnu is everywhere."

Pointing to a pillar in his throne room he asked, "Even in this pillar?"

Prahlad nodded, and the demon drew his sword and slashed at the column with all his strength. Instantly, **Narasingha** appeared and leaped toward the shocked demon.

Hiranya-kashipu attacked Narasingha like a wasp attacking a lion. The artist obviously appreciated Hiranya-kashipu's bravery in the face of certain death, so depicted him flying up at Narasingha, sword and shield raised, no fear on his face. Hiranya-kashipu and Narasingha occupy almost equal space on the canvas despite the difference in their size, and the artist has painted the weapons on a horizontal, giving a sense that the combatants are equally matched.

The lighting in the painting gives us a hint of the outcome, however. The combatants are illuminated in the foreground, along with the throne and the steps leading up to it in the background. Everything else is in shadow. The throne is crowned by a many-headed serpent, reminding us of Ananta Shesa, who frames Narasingha's head. Narasingha, who is already casting a long shadow on the steps leading up, will soon mount the throne.

Prahlad soothes Narasingha

Oil on canvas, 68 × 98 cm

The battle with **Hiranya-kashipu** did not last long. In one fluid motion **Narasingha** caught Hiranya-kashipu, just as a cat spears a mouse, bent him over his lap and, in the doorway of the assembly hall, tore him to pieces with his nails, pulling out the demon-king's intestines and hanging them like a macabre garland around his neck.

When Hiranya-kashipu died, his soldiers foolishly rushed forward and were dispatched. Their bodies litter the steps leading to the throne.

And what of the boon of immortality **Brahma** had granted Hiranya-kashipu? The boon was never violated. Hiranya-kashipu was killed neither by man nor beast but by Narasingha, half-man, half-beast. He was killed neither inside nor outside but on the threshold of the assembly hall. He died neither in the day nor at night but at twilight. The death occurred neither in the air nor on the earth but on Narasingha's lap. And Hiranya-kashipu was not killed by any weapon known to man but by Narasingha's naked claws.

Here we see the devas arriving on their swan airplanes to worship Narasingha, who descended to emancipate them from Hiranya-kashipu's reign. Hiranya-kashipu, on the strength of Brahma's boons, had upset dharma. With the demon-king's demise, the universal balance could be restored.

But even after the demon-king's death, Narasingha's eyes continued to blaze and his nostrils to flare in anger. No one could meet his gaze as he flexed his reddened claws and licked the sprinkled blood from his mouth and mane. All were afraid to approach him, even to praise him, and no one could pacify him. Even his eternal consort **Lakshmi** cowers at the foot of the steps.

But the small boy **Prahlad,** for whose protection Narasingha appeared, saw only his beloved **Vishnu** in the man-lion's form and was not afraid. Here we see Prahlad meekly climbing the steps, his hands folded in prayer. Seeing Prahlad's unshakable devotion, Narasingha's heart pooled with affection.

Narasingha then gave Prahlad lordship over the demons and returned to his eternal abode in the spiritual sky.

Ajamila

Oil on canvas, 50 × 62 cm

Ajamila was a pious brahmin who learned the power of divine grace and reciting God's name. His parents trained him in religious purity, but one day as a youth he witnessed a peasant embracing a prostitute. This sight, so rarely seen in that era, awoke his own lust, and as a result, Ajamila followed the prostitute and eventually married her. Together they had ten sons.

Gradually, he became addicted to alcohol and thievery. Still, he maintained a deep affection for his children, especially his youngest, whom he had named Narayana, a name for God.

When Ajamila lay on his deathbed at the age of eighty-eight, three Yamadutas, messengers of death, suddenly appeared at his bedside. Treacherous and ghastly, these hideous monsters began to tear his soul from his body so they could drag him to the hell he deserved. Here we see them grabbing hold of the subtle cord that binds the soul to the body and reeling it in like so much fishing line. One Yamaduta has his leg braced against the bed – few souls leave their bodies willingly – and another holds Ajamila's head down in a vicelike grip. The window behind the bed is barred, an indication of the imprisonment in hell that Ajamila is about to receive.

In his terror, Ajamila calls out for his son, Narayana, and we see Ajamila here surprised at the result. Though he hadn't intended to call God, the holy name Narayana touched his heart and he found himself remembering the original Narayana. Immediately, for each of the four syllables of the name, an emissary of Narayana (a Vishnuduta) rushed to his aid, each resembling his master and glowing with divinity.

In the scene in this painting, the lead Vishnuduta, his hand raised in a gesture of power and fearlessness, forbids the Yamadutas from taking Ajamila's soul and assures Ajamila of his protection. The Yamadutas look up from their work, shocked. No one has ever challenged them before.

The *Srimad-Bhagavatam* narration tells us that the Yamadutas and Vishnudutas then contended for Ajamila's soul, discussing both the particulars of his case and the general philosophical principles governing the after-death destinations of all kinds of souls. The story ends with Ajamila's life being extended. Devoting the rest of his days to meditation and yoga, he finally becomes a pure devotee of **Vishnu.** When death arrives for the second time, Ajamila has no worries: he has attained self-realization and is escorted by the Vishnudutas to the spiritual world.

JUDY KOSLOFSKY (JADURANI DEVI DASI)   1974

Diti seduces Kashyapa

Oil on canvas, 45 × 30 cm

Vishnu appears as both **Narasingha**, half-man, half-lion, and Varaha, the boar avatar. There is a common thread to both stories involving the seer Kashyapa and his wife Diti, granddaughter of **Brahma** (depicted in this painting). As we enter their world, Diti is jealous of her many sisters, all of whom have already given birth to children. Diti, however, is married to a yogi who takes his asceticism seriously. Here she attempts to seduce her husband in the middle of his spiritual practice with the hopes of begetting a child. Kashyapa will ultimately succumb to her desire.

But as mature practitioners of yoga, Kashyapa and Diti were expected to restrain themselves, especially during the *sandhya* (the juncture between day and night, or twilight), because to have sex at that time offends **Shiva,** who spends this time walking the earth with his followers. But Diti would not hear Kashyapa's request that she wait until dark. Here he maintains his yogic posture while Diti importunes him, leaning against his shoulder as she makes her case. Kashyapa sits before his sacred fire pit. Seeds are scattered around its perimeter, and Diti has knocked over the pot of clarified butter used in making oblations, causing the fire to suddenly billow clouds of ominous black smoke.

Diti will conceive twins. The two souls who will enter her womb are actually the gatekeepers cursed by the **Kumaras** and are therefore great devotees of Vishnu. (See "The Innocent Kumaras".) Still, due to the Kumaras' curse, they will incarnate as two of the world's most evil tyrants: Hiranya-kashipu, who is later killed by Narasingha, and his brother Hiran-yaksha, Varaha's demonic adversary.

However, a ray of light, like a ray of hope, cuts through the middle of the smoke cloud and illumines Diti's face. Because she comes to regret her inopportune seduction of her husband, Kashyapa will bless her that her grandson will be a great lover of Vishnu – the saintly boy **Prahlad.** Narasingha will appear for his protection.

> ## "Kindly bless me by fulfilling my desire. When someone in distress approaches a great person, his pleas should never go in vain."
>
> **Diti to Kashyapa**

Dhruva Fights Yaksha Magic

Oil on canvas, 60 × 45 cm

Dhruva was the son of the dynastic king Uttanapad. When he was a child, his stepmother insulted him and threatened to have him disinherited in favor of her own son. On his mother's advice, Dhruva left home to search for **Vishnu,** the desire burning in his heart to attain a kingdom even greater than that of the universal creator, **Brahma,** who was his great-grandfather. On his way he met **Narada,** who instructed him to practice yoga to gain Vishnu's favor. After only six months of intense practice, Vishnu appeared, resplendent, before him. Knowing the desires that had sent Dhruva into the forest to seek him, Vishnu not only granted him his father's throne but promised him at death rulership of the polestar, a spiritual planet in the material world. He also foretold his stepbrother's death at the hands of a Yaksha, a semi-divine being living in the Himalayan jungles.

Later, after Dhruva had become king, his brother was killed as predicted. Grief-stricken, Dhruva set out for the area where the Yakshas were known to dwell and, to avenge his brother's death, he boldly challenged the Yakshas to combat.

When it became clear to the Yakshas that they couldn't defeat Dhruva, they resorted to magic, as seen in this painting. The sky became overcast and foreboding. Then a blinding series of lightning bolts and thunderous rains crashed down, followed by a hail of severed body parts and weapons. Serpents and animals appeared to surround the noble Dhruva, and the sea itself seemed to surge up around him.

In the midst of this madness, Dhruva became confused. Sages came to his aid, reminding him of Vishnu and grounding him in reality. We can see them in this painting just behind Dhruva and to his left. Their words rekindled something deep inside him, and he drew on his experience with devotional meditation to clear his mind and win the battle.

In Western art, dark magical forces are usually depicted as bestial, monstrous, human-animal hybrids, their external forms reflecting their inner ugliness. But Yakshas are earthy creatures using earth magic, so the painter has used a more realistic brush to depict their illusions – although he has magnified the size of the creatures to give them power, and used color and lighting to evoke terror of nature gone awry. Here Dhruva stands out boldly, the sole light on the battlefield, his face calm and controlled. It's as if the showers of Yaksha illusions have washed Dhruva clean of doubt, and he now braces himself to dispel the magic with his golden-shafted arrows.

Gayatri

Oil on canvas, 90 × 70 cm

Gayatri is both goddess and sacred mantra. As a goddess she is mother of the Vedas. As a mantra her syllables sing **Krishna's** flutesong – his heart's call to every living being to return to him. In this painting we can trace the origin and descent of the mantra as it laces its way from Krishna's flute, circling into the eight ears of four-headed **Brahma** and encouraging him in his work of creation. Lotus-born Brahma then sings the mantra to his disciples in a perfect twelve-syllable meter, and it enters our world for our spiritual protection and upliftment.

The artist has hinted at the primary creation instigated by **Vishnu,** who is lying on the Causal Ocean. Brahma, who takes Vishnu's "blueprints" in the form of mantras and sets the worlds into motion, is sitting atop the lotus stemming from Vishnu's navel.

Gayatri, the main figure in the painting, is depicted in her goddess form. The swan at her feet represents Saraswati, goddess of learning, and symbolizes creation, of which the Gayatri mantra is the catalyzing force. The swan, often used as a symbol in Vedic iconography, is said to possess the unique ability to separate pure milk from a mixture of milk and water – similar to the mystic's ability to recognize and serve the one Source in a pluralistic world.

Gayatri is four-handed. In one of her hands she holds a sacred rosary for chanting Krishna's names, signifying that meditation on God's name is a necessary part of spiritual practice. In another she holds a water pot, symbolizing the simple, self-contained life of one who has vowed to follow the flute-song back to its source. In a third she holds a lotus, symbol of living in this world without being of it, and in her fourth she holds the sacred texts of the Vedas.

Invoking the Gayatri mantra takes us back to the scene at the top of the painting – and the invitation to join **Radha** and Krishna in the spiritual world where they are enjoying unending pastimes of love in a beautiful pastoral setting.

The Three Lives of Bharata

Oil on canvas, 40 × 30 cm

The story of Bharata's three lives appears in the *Srimad-Bhagavatam* to instruct readers on karma, reincarnation, and the importance of directing our thoughts productively at death.

In the first of Bharata's lives, he is a great king. After a lifetime of executing his royal duties, he retired to the forest, like his father before him, to absorb his mind in **Vishnu** by practicing penance and meditating on the **Gayatri** mantra.

But one day he saw a pregnant deer leap across the Gandaki River in fear of a pursuing tiger and drop her fawn into the swirling waters. The doe's heart gave out just before she could swim to the other side, and Bharata scooped the orphaned fawn from the river. His heart full of compassion, he decided to raise the fawn himself.

As the fawn grew and began to playfully nudge him with its velvet nose as he sat in meditation, Bharata found his spiritual contemplations replaced by thoughts of the fawn and its enchanting frolicking. Gradually, his spiritual practices became less and less absorbing as his concentration on his animal friend grew.

When death claimed Bharata, his mind was focused not on his spiritual progress but on the welfare of the deer. These thoughts carried him to his next body – the body of a deer. The painting here shows Bharata at the moment of death. He has fallen into what appears to be a dry riverbed, symbolic of the dried-up river of his spiritual ecstasies and forgotten penances. The moon rises overhead, representing the eye of Vishnu, witness to all our desires. While Bharata throws his arm pitifully over the deer, which cannot save him and will itself again be orphaned, we see Bharata's soul rising up, an old man, entering into the ethereal body of a fawn.

The story goes on: because the bulk of his life as King Bharata was spent dutifully and in spiritual concerns, he was blessed to remember his past life even while in the deer's body. Thus he was able to realize his mistake. His resolve to attain his original spiritual goal reawakened and strengthened, and during his existence as a deer he returned to the hermitage of sages near whom he had lived in his previous incarnation, to listen to their discourses and kirtan.

Finally, when death again visited Bharata, his mind was focused on Vishnu and he took his third birth as the pure brahmin saint, **Jada Bharata.** Jada Bharata's story is told on the following spread.

Jada Bharata

Oil on canvas, 52 × 40 cm

King **Bharata**, who became a deer in his next life, took his third birth as Jada Bharata, or "Dull" Bharata, a social outcaste who appeared unable to function in the world into which he was born. But Jada Bharata was not dull; he was God-intoxicated. His memory of his two previous lives made him vigilant in his meditation, and to protect himself from distraction, he remained silent. His complete absorption in the divine made him appear disengaged with everything around him, and he did not bind himself by the values nor bother himself with the troubles that defined others' lives.

This posed a problem for his family and neighbors. His brahmin father tried to educate him but found him unteachable. Because he never spoke, people in his village tormented him. After his parents died, his stepbrothers mocked and mistreated him.

One night they ordered him to guard a rice paddy field. Worshipers of Goddess Kali found him alone and decided to sacrifice him to the goddess. Jada Bharata went with them willingly; life and death were the same to him. Remembering the misstep that had led him into the body of a deer, he wanted only to focus his mind and heart on **Krishna** without deviation.

The Kali worshipers were pleased to find such a compliant victim. They bathed and garlanded him, and anointed him with fragrant oils to prepare him for the sacrifice. Just as the priest was about to behead Bharata, however, the goddess leaped out of the deity standing on the altar and saved Bharata's life.

The event in this painting takes place later in Jada Bharata's life. He did not return home after his brush with the Kali worshipers, but left to wander around on his own. Here, he has met King Rahugana. The king, short of a palanquin bearer and seeing what appeared to be a disheveled but young and strong beggar by the side of the road, thought him fit to carry the load. Although the great soul Jada Bharata should have been enlightening others, not carrying palanquins, he kept himself hidden, like a light under a basket, and the king misjudged him and pressed him into his service.

But Jada Bharata didn't give the king a smooth ride. His awareness of the soul in all beings made him avoid trampling ants on the path, and as he moved this way and that he jostled the palanquin. Rahugana threatened to have him beaten. Finally, Bharata turned to the king and spoke spiritual truth, and Raghugana recognized him as an illumined soul. Under Bharata's counsel, King Rahugana relinquished his pride and also took to the spiritual path.

Priyavrata Thwarts Night

Oil on canvas, 46 × 61 cm

Priyavrata, powerful emperor of an earlier age, didn't like that only half the universe was illuminated by sunlight during the day while the other half experienced night. According to ancient Vedic astronomy, the sun moves for six months on the northern side of the universal axis, Mount Sumeru, and for six months on Sumeru's southern side. We experience this north-south divide on earth too: when it's winter in the northern hemisphere, it's summer in the southern.

Priyavrata wanted to increase the abundance of all beings by providing them more hours of daylight, so he devised a chariot that was as brilliant as the sun and followed the sun around Mount Sumeru. While the sun was illuminating the universe's northern hemisphere, Priyavrata was illuminating the southern, effectively abolishing night.

It is said that the light he brought was as pleasing as moon rays in the spring and provided more warmth than sunshine in the fall. Still, **Brahma** feared an ecological imbalance and asked Priyavrata to stop.

When Priyavrata drove his chariot behind the sun, the rims of his chariot wheels created impressions that later became seven oceans, dividing the world into seven continents. The king gave one of these continents to each of his seven sons and retired to the forest to live as an ascetic.

In this painting we see Priyavrata circling Mount Sumeru. According to the *Mahabharata,* Sumeru is round like the morning sun and shines brilliantly. The sun and moon circumambulate it daily, and the Pleaides rises and sets on it. Sumeru supports the heavens like the pole of a giant golden parasol. In Vedic cosmography, Sumeru is given almost equal importance to the polestar, which is considered the pivot around which all the planets and stars revolve. Sumeru's gardens are filled with fragrant flowers and fruit, and the air is fresh and pure. Everywhere are shining palaces of gold, and the devas, celestial musicians, and heavenly dancers play there.

The Vedic culture is extremely ancient, and archaeological evidence points to the idea that it was once spread all over the world. The idea of a universal axis like Sumeru is common to many ancient cultures, including those of Egypt, India, China, Greece, Mesopotamia, and a number of the tribal societies in ancient Africa and the Americas. Mount Sumeru is said to be the home of the devas – and a mountain home for the gods in the center of the universe is also typical of many cultures.

saubhari muni

Oil on canvas, 68 × 48 cm

Saubhari Muni was a powerful and serious yogi who, as a young man and looking for a place to practice meditation undisturbed, entered deep into the water of a river. He sat in the relative silence of that river for years, mastering the chanting of mantras and deepening his mysticism.

Years into his underwater meditation, Saubhari saw two fish copulating and felt a surprising desire for sexual pleasure awaken. By now he was old, but he emerged from the river and approached the king to ask for one of his fifty daughters in marriage.

Saubhari was long-haired and ugly from his years underwater, and his body had become greenish from the algae. Still, mystic yogis were powerful people, and the king didn't want to risk being cursed by one, so he said, "My daughters may marry whomever they choose. If one of my daughters chooses you, I give you my blessings."

Saubhari saw himself in the king's hesitation. He was feeble from old age. His hair was gray, his skin slack, and his head trembled. He also knew that women didn't like to marry yogis, since that meant living in the forest with nothing but roots and fruits to eat. Saubhari decided to use his yogic power to rejuvenate his body and make himself desirable. When the fifty princesses saw the handsome young man who then came before them, they *all* agreed to marry him.

And that's when the trouble started. After the marriage, the princesses stopped treating one another as sisters and became rivals instead. Saubhari had no peace. To satisfy them (and perhaps to keep them apart), he used mantras to create a palatial home, with parks and lakes and flower-filled gardens. Saubhari created so much wealth that the king, who was extremely wealthy in his own right, became embarrassed by his own relative poverty.

But over time Saubhari realized that sex and wealth didn't satisfy the fire of desire that burned in him. Instead of quenching the fire, he was drizzling oil into it. He yearned for his quiet river bottom. He decided to renounce everything, and, taking his wives, he returned to the forest for a life of renewed austerity.

One day while he was alone, he remembered what had driven him from his meditation in the first place. How could watching fish mate have led him to this point? He had lost his spiritual viewpoint, and with it, his power of austerity, spiritual beauty, and happiness. Saubhari then focused his yoga on serving **Vishnu.** Gradually, he was able to peel back the gross and subtle material bodies until there was nothing left of him but pure soul.

Indra Battles Jambha

Oil on canvas, 50 × 72 cm

This painting depicts the fight between Indra, lord of the devas, riding his war elephant, and the demon Jambha, on his lion mount. Deva and demon, good and evil, are in a constant battle for supremacy in the universe. Sometimes the devas, lords of light, win, and at other times they are overpowered. When the devas are overcome, it's usually for one of three reasons: they have committed a moral transgression, which has weakened them; the demons have successfully performed a sacrifice and tipped the scales of power in their favor; or all-powerful time, representative of the Supreme, has decreed it. It was Indra's moral transgression that led to this battle.

Once, sage Durvasa was passing on the road and saw Indra in procession riding on his elephant. Feeling magnanimous, Durvasa took the garland of flowers from around his neck and offered it to Indra as a blessing. Indra, however, accepted the garland carelessly, and in his pride placed it on the trunk of his elephant. The elephant then threw the garland to the ground and crushed it under its feet. This simple offense shattered the peace of the world.

Of all the sages, Durvasa is the most volatile, and he cursed Indra to lose his wealth and position. Since the devas and demons were at war at the time, the devas found themselves defeated by the demons.

So the devas went to **Brahma,** the creator god, for advice. When Brahma saw the devas bereft of influence and strength, he understood that the three worlds were in trouble. To find a solution, Brahma then concentrated his mind on the Supreme Person, **Vishnu.**

Vishnu advised the devas to declare a truce with the demons; they should work with the demons in the common cause of finding the elixir of immortality and then share it between them. The demons agreed to this, and hostilities ceased. But when the elixir was actually found, the demons tried to steal it for themselves. Vishnu tricked them, however, and gave the elixir to the devas, at which point the demons again declared war.

Returning to the scene of this painting, Indra has just defeated the king of the demons, Bali. The powerful Jambha, in his attempt to avenge his king and friend, strikes Indra on the shoulder with his club and then attacks Indra's elephant. The elephant has just touched its knees to the ground and collapsed. Seeing his rival's ferocity, Indra is inflamed with anger. In a moment he will mount his chariot, drawn by a thousand horses, and throw his thunderbolt at Jambha, severing his head from his body.

Yama, the Death God

Oil on canvas, 59 × 88 cm

When the demon Hiranyaksha was destroyed by Varaha, no one grieved more than **Hiranya-kashipu,** the demon's elder brother. Still, at a funeral service in honor of Hiranyaksha, Hiranya-kashipu spoke eloquently about the difference between body and soul and tried to pacify the departed demon's sons.

In his eulogy, he told the ancient story of King Suyajna, who was also killed in battle, and how Yama, king of the underworld, once appeared before his grieving widows in the form of a young boy to ease their pain.

Two thirds of the canvas is taken up by Suyajna and his grieving wives. A number of his wives have loosened their hair in mourning, and a sage stands behind with his assistant, chanting mantras to smooth the soul's passage. The fallen king's helmet has rolled from his head. His turban, now the color of mud, unravels. A Vedic king's turban signifies his dignity, and his crown his authority. Here in death, both are lost.

The king's sword lies to the side. Swords are associated with fire and life; for a warrior they signify independence, self-respect, power, and the marriage between spiritual and temporal responsibilities. They were used to protect the weak and oppressed. But Suyajna's sword has been cut in half. His quiver of arrows and a broken spear, too, lay nearby. This suggests he was a great king and protector, but that he is no longer able to protect even the grieving women who surround him. The chariot wheel to Yama's left represents the wheel of time, which crushes without mercy all our dreams.

Yama has come to this desolate battlefield to instruct the queens. It is he who has taken their husband on God's behalf and who will explain to them the difference between body and soul, freeing them from fear of himself, the death god. It's interesting that here Yama appears as a child, but with his chest bound by a warrior's hard breast band.

The painter has captured something Yama himself will point out: the self-absorption a relative's grief brings on. Here the queens lament the passing of one man, while others lie nearby with no one to lament them. Two men pull a body by its legs to the collective funeral pyre at the far side of the field.

Rama's victory party

Oil on canvas, 56 × 45 cm

Among **Krishna's** many avatars, few are as well-known as Rama, whose story is told in the epic *Ramayana*. Rama stands central in this painting – a true hero – tall, strong, righteous, his skin a glowing emerald.

This painting depicts Rama's moment of triumph as he returns to reclaim his throne after having killed the demon **Ravana.** A victory arch rises over the party's head. But Rama does not look joyful. Rather, he stands in the *abhanga* pose, indicating that he is deep in thought. At the same time, his left hand, palm up, fingertips down, blesses all those who have surrendered to his rule.

By his side stands his beloved wife, Sita, emblem of chastity and all that is good and true. Sita is the goddess of fortune, and the artist has depicted her carrying a water pot, indicating abundance, wisdom, fertility, and immortality.

Rama and Sita are accompanied by Rama's younger brothers. Bharata, dressed like an ascetic, stands to Rama's right. Bharata's mother was instrumental in having Rama banished from his kingdom on the day of his coronation so Bharata could rule. Bharata refused to accept the throne, however, and remained outside the city during Rama's exile, worshipping his brother's sandals. We see him standing next to Rama, ready to return the sandals – and the rule – to his brother. Shatrughna, another of Rama's brothers, stands behind Bharata, waving a white whisk.

Hanuman, the famous monkey-warrior, kneels at Rama's feet, holding the royal umbrella at the ready, and the monkey-king Sugriva, armed with a saber, kneels just behind Sita.

All eyes are on Rama except Lakshman's. Always alert and at Rama's side, here Lakshman seems to look out from the painting as if to challenge anyone who might pose a danger to Rama or Sita.

Note the South Indian *makaras*, or "sea-dragons," on either side of the steps. A *makara* is a hybrid grouping of animals, and most have the jaws of a crocodile, the trunk and feet of an elephant, the sharp scales and flexible body of a shark, the shifting eyes of a monkey, the tusks of a boar, and a peacock's fantail. They often edge archways around deity altars, symbolizing the deity's power to decide over life and death. Perhaps the contemplative look we find on Rama's face in this painting is just this: his awareness of the weight of his responsibility as he gazes out at his kingdom for the first time in fourteen years.

Rama Kills Ravana

Oil on canvas, 310 × 415 cm

Ravana, seen hurtling from the sky here, has ten heads and twenty arms, signifying his scholarship in the ten primary Vedic texts and almost unparalleled status as a warrior. Ravana could command both conventional and magical weapons. He was also a great king. Yet Ravana used neither his knowledge nor his power to protect others. Instead, he became a man-eater.

The *Ramayana* tells how Ravana kidnapped **Rama's** wife, Sita, and how, after creating an alliance with an army of monkey-warriors, Rama set out to get her back. The monkeys engulfed Ravana's fortified city, battling his soldiers in hand-to-hand combat. Great heroes from both sides fought, and there were thousands of fatalities. One by one, however, the great man-eating chieftains, including a number of Ravana's own sons and his beloved but monstrous brother, fell before the power of the heroes on the other side.

This painting depicts the last day of the battle and the moment Rama kills Ravana. Rama had already tried to kill Ravana by severing each of his ten heads, but when he learned that Ravana had obtained a boon protecting his heads, Rama invoked the magical *brahmastra* weapon and aimed it at Ravana's black heart. Rama's arrow looks almost puny in relation to the gigantic demon, but it entered Ravana's heart with such force that it passed through his body and struck the earth behind him. Here we see the many-headed Ravana tumbling from the sky, his faces masks of pain and outrage. His city burns in the background. The artist has painted the dark Ravana with his black cape flying up like a bat's wing against the only lighted patch of sky, while an effulgent Rama stands on a hillock, untouched by the gloom. Rama is masterful and in control as he shoots his devastating arrow.

The *brahmastra* is the personal weapon of **Brahma.** The same Brahma who gave Ravana the boon that he would not be killed by beast or god (Rama came in the form of a man, because Ravana had neglected to ask for protection against men) actually supplied the weapon that killed him.

Hanuman

Oil on canvas, 60 × 45 cm

Hanuman is a Vanara, a member of the race of "forest dwellers" – half-human, half-monkey beings – who lived in the jungles of South India. Those who are familiar with the *Ramayana* will recognize Hanuman as **Rama's** greatest devotee.

Rama meets Hanuman for the first time when he is searching for his kidnapped wife, Sita. As soon as the two meet, a deep love springs up between them, and Hanuman's soliloquies in glorification of Rama are perhaps the most beautiful expressions of devotion and surrender in the world's spiritual literature.

The *Ramayana* tells us that it was Hanuman who leaped from the tip of South India to **Ravana's** island kingdom of Sri Lanka – a distance of thirty-one kilometers – to search for Sita. Sita was indeed there, and after assuring her that he would bring Rama to rescue her, Hanuman then battled Ravana's minions. After doing away with several of the strongest, Hanuman allowed himself to be captured; he wanted to deliver an ultimatum to Ravana: return Sita to Rama or prepare for battle. Ravana was so incensed by Hanuman's words that he ordered Hanuman's tail set on fire. Hanuman then escaped and used his lit tail to set Ravana's golden city ablaze.

An acrobatic Hanuman leaps gracefully back across the sea in this painting, his face noble, his hand held out in a graceful gesture. The mace resting on his shoulder looks almost like a drum major's baton, and we sense that Hanuman has danced nimbly through the streets even as he wreaked havoc among the demons.

The artist has painted Hanuman red in commemoration of another event in Hanuman's life. Later, when the battle with Ravana is over and Rama and Sita are ruling peacefully in Ayodhya, Hanuman sees Sita applying *sindoor* to the part in her hair. *Sindoor* is a red powder symbolizing life and strength, and married women use it to give strength and energy to their husbands. When Sita explained to Hanuman that wearing *sindoor* would give Rama a long life, Hanuman doused himself in the red powder. In return for his devotion, Rama blessed Hanuman with immortality and eternal youth.

Ravana was so incensed by Hanuman's words that he ordered Hanuman's tail set on fire.

samudra satisfies Rama

Oil on canvas, 70 × 50 cm

To rescue Sita, who was being held on the island of demons, **Rama** had to cross the ocean. He therefore went with his Vanara army to the ocean's shore to think about how to get his entire army across. He decided to appeal to Samudra, the ocean deva, and sitting on a mat of sacred kusha grass, he began to fast to attract Samudra's attention. But after three days of fasting, the ocean god did not appear, and Rama, in his impatience to rescue Sita, became frustrated. He turned to his brother and said, "Just see the vanity of this deva. Although I have sat here humbly beseeching him, he has not appeared. Forbearance, gentleness, and polite speech are usually construed as weaknesses by the wicked, and the world regards with respect only those who are arrogant, harsh, and given to meting out strong punishments. I shall therefore dry up the ocean with my bow and flaming arrows, and my army may then walk across the seabed to Lanka."

Rama then strung his bow and, his eyes red with anger, began to shoot hundreds of fiery arrows into the water. The ocean roared and rose up in response. Clouds of steam covered its surface as the flaming arrows pierced the water.

A chastened Samudra made his appearance. Rising out of the ocean like a dawning sun, he folded his hands before Rama and said, "Every element has its natural state, O Rama. It is my nature to be fathomless and unfordable. But I will tell you how your army may cross. The Vanara Nala should lead the construction of a bridge over my waters. I will sustain it. Go to the abode of Ravana, O hero. Kill him and regain Sita. My water will present no impediment. On seeing your uncommon deed, all great heroes and kings in the future will glorify you."

In this impressionistic painting, the artist has played with the balance of warm and cool tones to beautifully capture the spirit of the ocean deva's apology. There is no anger left either in Rama's face or the serene late afternoon sky above him, and as he steps off the rocks into the water to greet Samudra, who stands in a mosaic of color, we no longer see Rama as the petitioner of the devas but as their master.

The ocean roared and rose up in response. Clouds of steam covered its surface as the flaming arrows pierced the water.

KEVIN YEE (RAMADASA ABHIRAMA DASA)

Rama Returns to Ayodhya

Oil on canvas, 88 × 117 cm

After **Ravana** kidnapped Sita and **Rama** waged a great war to win her back, Rama and Sita returned to their happy kingdom of Ayodhya. The royal couple and their associates (here, **Hanuman** and Sugriva, leaders of the monkey-warriors, and Lakshman, Rama's brother) disembark from a swan airplane, the artist's imaginative interpretation of the famed Pushpaka chariot. This aerial car was originally gifted to Kuvera, treasurer of the devas, later stolen by Ravana, then inherited by Ravana's one surviving brother, and now given as a gift to Rama to speed his homeward journey. According to the *Ramayana,* the Pushpaka could go anywhere at will and was as brilliant as the sun.

The chariot has alighted on the bank of the Sarayu River. Rama's waiting marble palace shimmers across the water. The party first greets the chief queen and Rama's mother, Kaushalya, whom we see rising from her chair, her lady-in-waiting gesturing as if to say, "See, Lady, your lost son has indeed come home after his fourteen years in exile." Lakshman's mother Sumitra also rises from behind Kaushalya's throne, while male servants bow to their master returned. A group of citizens watch the reunion from the side.

The artist has taken some liberties in this painting in order to highlight the great joy Rama's family members felt on his return. Rama and Lakshman are bare-chested as befits those who have been living simple lives in the forest, but Sita has donned peacock silk in lieu of the bark cloth she wore throughout her exile. The queens and their attendants are also dressed lavishly, even though while Rama was away they have become widows. Indian artists traditionally paint the queens at Rama's return wearing no ornaments and dressed only in the simple white of mourning. Yet here we see sunny yellows, sky blues, and rich purples and reds – colors that speak of happiness and pride. Kaikeyi, the queen who caused Rama's banishment and, as a result, her husband's death due to grief, is conspicuous by her absence.

> **"See, your lost son has indeed come home after his fourteen years in exile."**

Kardama's Aerial Mansion

Oil on canvas, 50 × 40 cm

Ancient Vedic texts described *vimanas,* flying machines, long before modern science had the technology to develop its own. In the story depicted in this painting, the sage Kardama Muni, anxious to please his wife, Devahuti, who had given up her wealth and status as an emperor's daughter to serve him in a forest hermitage, used his yogic power to create a massive flying city controlled by his will.

This city was magnificent; the walls and streets were bedecked with precious and semi-precious stones. The central palace was surrounded by beautiful trees and colorful gardens filled with the buzzing of bees. The palace's beauty was enhanced by coral daises and gold pinnacles crowning sapphire domes. Its walls were alive with engravings and sculptures. The floors were made of shiny emeralds, while the choicest rubies tiled the area surrounding the compound.

This is a lavish gift even for a beloved wife, and Devahuti appears awed by it. As the two stand opposite, mirroring one another, we feel the peace between them nurtured from years of equal austerity, service, and love. Doves fly overhead and flowers grow in the space between the two, suggesting harmony.

Kardama and Devahuti will leave the forest of their early married life and travel in this aerial mansion to the gardens of the devas. There, Devahuti will give birth to nine daughters and one son, **Kapila,** an avatar of **Krishna.**

Seeking to please his beloved wife, the sage Kardama exercised his yogic power and instantly produced an aerial mansion that could travel at his will. It was a wonderful structure, bedecked with all sorts of jewels, adorned with pillars of precious stones, and capable of yielding whatever one desired.

King Puranjana

Oil on canvas, 60 × 45 cm

The story of King Puranjana, as graphically described by this painting, was told to King Prachini by sage **Narada** after the king had submitted himself as a disciple at the sage's feet. Puranjana literally means "one who enjoys the body," and the tale is a parable about the woes of worldly attachment and bodily identification. Puranjana is the Everyman, for everyone tries to enjoy his or her physical life with unbridled enthusiasm.

King Puranjana had a well-wishing friend, but didn't know anything about him – not even his name. Nonetheless, Puranjana went about his business like most people do, his friend accompanying him. He looked for a place to live, but couldn't find anything suitable until he traveled south of the Himalayas. There he found a palace with nine gateways that attracted him. In a nearby garden there was even a woman who held his interest. This beautiful woman had ten attendants, and each attendant had a hundred wives.

The allegory continues, and when it is over, Narada explains it. Puranjana is the self, and the unknown friend the **Indweller,** who accompanies the soul in its sojourn through material existence even though we are mostly ignorant of his presence. The palace in which Puranjana finally finds comfort is the human body, and the nine gateways the nine openings of the body. The young woman who captures his interest is his intelligence, for everyone is entranced by his own mind. Her ten male attendants are the five organs of perception and the five organs of action, and the attendants' one hundred wives are the desires that blossom from the interaction between the mind, intelligence, and senses.

In this painting we see Puranjana at death, his frightened soul bound like an animal and reaching back toward his dying body. The artist has set Puranjana's body aflame to indicate that he suffered from fever during his death throes. An angry jackal, stag, and boar prepare to attack – all animals Puranjana has killed while hunting. (We can just see Puranjana's arrows still protruding from their bodies.) The five-headed serpent-guardian of his city – his vital energy – has been captured and is being forced out of the body after the soul, while the citizens – Puranjana's many actions and karmic reactions – walk in the gloom behind, bound to follow the soul who created and supported them. Time personified whips his soldiers forward, and the witch of old age stands to the side, gloating.

shiva Meditates on Rama

Oil on canvas, 70 × 50 cm

Shiva, whose name means "auspicious," is the god of destruction and one of **Krishna's** greatest devotees. Here, we see him in deep meditation on Krishna's avatar, **Rama.** Though Rama was devoted to Shiva in his pastimes, Shiva worships his source, Rama.

The most common image of Shiva shows him as beautiful, three-eyed, and crowned with the crescent moon. The **Ganges** flows from his matted hair, white as milk. His skin is gray because he smears his body with ashes from crematorium fires, and his throat is blue because of the poison he drank when the milk ocean was churned. He is decorated by a garland of cobras, indicating his mastery over *kundalini,* the yogic power of controlling the spiritual energy coiled at the base of the spine. The cobra also signifies the eternal cycling of time and, because snakes shed their skin without dying, they are an ancient symbol of reincarnation.

Shiva's long matted hair tells us that he is an ascetic, and the cooling crescent moon on his brow reminds us of the inevitability of time, which destroys all in its wake. The hourglass-shaped *damaru* drum, seen here hanging from his trident, vibrates with the power of creation. It is significant that Shiva has chosen to suspend his drum from his trident, which with its long shaft symbolizes the universal axis. The tiger skin on which he sits shows his seriousness in yoga practice and connects him to Shakti, the goddess – his wife – who rides a tiger. Shiva's third eye, representing his higher consciousness, is open and alert, even as his other two eyes are closed in concentration. Rudraksha beads adorn his neck and arms.

Shiva sits under the great leafy canopy of a sacred banyan tree. Banyans are considered eternal because of their ability to grow roots from their branches and thus expand themselves almost endlessly. They are also evergreens and so firmly rooted that they can withstand hot sun, monsoon rains, and high winds. For centuries, gurus and their disciples have built their ashrams and schools under banyan trees, and Indian village councils still meet under them today.

The artist has painted Rama's face at the top of what appears to be a pillar of light, suggesting that Shiva's meditation is enlightened enough to illumine the face of God. Rama himself seems composed, his features almost Buddhistic and his hair seemingly composed of the matted banyan branches. This may suggest that Shiva is meditating on Rama during Rama's forest exile.

surabhi, "The Fragrant"

Oil on canvas, 70 × 50 cm

According to Vedic cosmography, just as our world has oceans of water, other worlds have oceans filled with other liquids. One such ocean – birthplace of the luminous moon – is filled with milk. The milk ocean figures prominently in Vedic creation stories as well as in a number of stories relating to the interaction between devas and demons. In one such episode early in the universe's history, the gods and demons establish a truce and together churn the milk ocean to gain the elixir of immortality. But before the elixir appears, a variety of creatures is churned from the ocean's depths, each making its entrance into our world for the first time. The first of these creatures is Surabhi, the original cow.

Surabhis are spiritual creatures – it is the *surabhi* cows that are so lovingly tended by **Krishna** in the spiritual world – and they have the mystical ability to fulfill desires.

The cow in this painting has just left an ideal world to enter this one immediately after its creation. In Vedic culture cows are seen as motherly and magnanimous; they give their milk to human children as willingly as to their own calves. But it is a somber cow who greets us here as she steps daintily from the ocean. She seems to be looking out at the young world not with optimism but with resignation. It is a solitary look. It's as if she has already taken stock of the pain and labor and conflict of this world and accepted it. Still, she swishes her tail, giving the viewer a sense of a noble and generous spirit – one prepared to fully enter this new place despite its problems and to perform her dharma. Dharma is the support that harmonizes a complex world.

And what is her dharma? Surabhi will give her milk to the sages who perform the Vedic sacrifices that ensure harmony between all creatures. When Surabhi appeared, therefore, the wise among both the devas and demons greeted her with enthusiasm and immediately milked her, turning her milk into clarified butter, a necessary oblation in their holy sacrificial fires.

Surabhis are spiritual creatures, and they have the mystical ability to fulfill desires.

DOUG BALL (PARIKSIT DASA)   1976

Shiva Drinks Halahala Poison

Oil on canvas, 60 × 45 cm

After the devas were defeated by the demons in a cosmic struggle, the devas made a truce with the demons so they could churn the ocean of milk and share the elixir of immortality. On **Vishnu's** order, the devas and demons used Mount Mandara as a churning rod and the giant serpent Vasuki as a rope. When the mountain began to sink beneath the waves, Vishnu appeared as the divine tortoise avatar, Kurma, and held it on his back. Even with Kurma's support, however, the mountain listed, so Vishnu took another form, and we see him balancing the mountain while sitting atop it with his thousand arms.

Still, the work was hard, and the devas and demons were soon exhausted. Vasuki, stretched by the churning, was close to death. So Vishnu, who is the source of all energy, infused each of them with the vigor and enthusiasm to continue.

As the devas and demons churned with renewed strength, the ocean suddenly yielded its first product: the dangerous *halahala* poison. The poison flowed from the milk ocean's waves as froth and spread in all directions, posing a threat to the new creation. The devas approached **Shiva** for help.

Shiva, whose name means "auspicious," said, "It is my duty to protect all living beings. Devas, demons, and all other creatures forget their own true natures and are therefore always afraid of death. I have not forgotten myself, so let me be compassionate. Even at the risk of my own life, let me drink this poison so all beings may be happy because of me."

Shiva then reduced the poison to a palmful and sipped it without swallowing it. The poison was so virulent, however, that it marked Shiva's neck with a bluish line where he held it in his throat, and he has since been known as Nilakantha, "the blue-throated one." Scorpions, cobras, and other animals whose bites or stings are poisonous, along with poisonous plants, licked up whatever drops of poison fell from Shiva's hand and increased their own venom. These creatures are seen at Shiva's feet in this painting.

> **"O greatest of all demigods, please save us from this fiery poison, which is spreading all over the three worlds."**

JÜRGEN WILMS (AJATASHATRU DASA)   1982

shiva and His Followers

Oil on canvas, 50 × 57 cm

Shiva is master of *tamas,* ignorance. In English, ignorance simply means a lack of knowledge, but *tamas,* its Sanskrit equivalent, is a more colorful word that connotes darkness, gloom, losing one's way, depression, lack of self-awareness, and illusion. In its expanded, cosmic sense, *tamas* is the cause of everything heavy in this world – dullness, lust, anger, pride, and sorrow. It is a quality of matter, and along with matter's other two qualities – *rajas* (passion) and *sattva* (purity, truth) – it twines and twists into innumerable shapes, emotions, and events. When *tamas* is predominant, we can expect imbalance and violence, indolence and death. The three modes, as they're known, are comparable to the three states of human consciousness – *sattva* is the intellectual sphere, *rajas* the emotional, and *tamas,* the grossest of the three, the purely physical.

As the master of *tamas,* Shiva is not subject to it, yet he feels compassion for those who are attracted to and ultimately overcome by it. These are the spirits that surround him in this painting – the ghosts of those who died violent deaths, the witches and cannibals, the vampires and black sorcerers, and the troubled spirits of all those who have neither been liberated nor reborn in a physical body. Because these beings are subtle, they are not bound by the confines of a physical body and can take whatever fearful form they like, and we see here animals and lizards with fiery eyes. A haloed Shiva riding his bull leads them forward. It is said that out of his kindness, he wanders the earth with his followers when day meets night so he can help them leave their suffering, ghostly existence and find opportunities for a suitable rebirth. One of the greatest forms of pain is to live as a subtle being, filled with desires, but with no body through which to satisfy them.

The artist has elevated Shiva and his entourage above the landscape to show that they travel the pathways between heaven and earth. Prominent in this painting is Nandi, Shiva's bull. Bulls the world over symbolize sex and lust. Most living beings are controlled by their sex impulse, which at its basest level is a selfish drive for physical gratification and so under the sway of *tamas.* But Shiva rides the bull – he has mastered lust – and this makes him a suitable leader for all those who have become lost in selfishness and ignorance.

shiva counsels His wife, sati

Oil on canvas, 63 × 49 cm

Sati, daughter of **Daksha,** is an avatar of the supreme goddess **Radha,** and the eternal shakti, or energy, of **Shiva.** Later, she will reappear as Parvati, the gentlest face of the goddess.

Sati is renowned for her great love for her husband. She is young in this painting, and Shiva, despite his youthful appearance, is ancient. Sati's father has almost disowned her because of an insult he imagined his son-in-law gave him, and it has been a long time since Sati has visited her parental home. But her father is a progenitor, an important dignitary in the universe, and he is holding a religious sacrifice to which he has invited all the important people – all, that is, except Shiva. Sati rationalizes her father's neglect by saying that formal invitations are not necessary for family members. Shiva knows better.

Here we see Sati almost pouting. She wants to attend her father's sacrifice – it's an opportunity to see her mother and sisters, whom she rarely sees anymore – but how can she go without her husband? Shiva speaks to her here, his hand raised in a teaching gesture as he explains the temporary nature of family relationships and warns her that she will suffer a slight at her father's hands should she choose to attend the sacrifice. He fears the insult will be greater than she can bear.

Sati is already wearing the white cloth usually reserved for grieving and renounced women, foreshadowing future events. That she also wears her gold ornaments, however, beautifying herself in her husband's presence, suggests that it will not be her husband whom she renounces.

> **"My dear beautiful wife, you have said that one may go to a friend's house without being invited, and this is true, provided such a friend does not find fault with the guest because of bodily identification and thereby become angry toward him."**
>
> **Shiva to Sati**

virabhadra Beheads Daksha

Oil on canvas, 55 × 30 cm

This painting continues the story from the last spread. There we saw **Sati** about to attend her father's sacrifice, although she and her husband had not been invited. **Shiva** had feared that Sati's father, **Daksha,** would insult her due to her relationship with her husband. He was correct. Not able to bear her father's insult, Sati had told Daksha, "I shall no longer bear the unworthy body you gave me. If someone has eaten poisoned food, it's best to vomit." Then, after praising her husband to the assembly, Sati had immolated herself in a blaze of yogic fire.

When Shiva heard of Sati's death and that Daksha had done nothing to prevent it, his anger could not be contained. He ripped out a strand of his hair – a strand that vibrated with electric potency – and dashed it to the ground. Laughing like a madman, Shiva watched as this strand grew into a vicious demon, ugly and powerful, with vampirelike teeth and flaming red hair. His name was Virabhadra, and he had thousands of arms (the artist has painted only eight), each equipped with a deadly weapon. He garlanded himself with a lei of human heads.

Fearsome though the demon was, he humbly approached Shiva, his master, and asked, "What would you have me do?" Shiva in-stalled him as the chief of his soldiers and gave him his first order: kill Daksha and his soldiers.

Many of Shiva's soldiers followed Virabhadra, who marched off with a tumultuous roar. Virabhadra carried a great trident, powerful enough to kill death. In this painting, Virabhadra has already desecrated the sacrificial arena where Daksha was about to offer oblations, and killed or maimed many of the sacrifice's participants. We see him here with Daksha in his great hand. He will decapitate him on the instrument used for sacrificing goats.

Virabhadra saw the wooden device in the sacrificial arena by which the animals were to have been killed. He took the opportunity of this facility to behead Daksha.

Daksha surrenders to shiva

Oil on canvas, 42 × 36 cm

After Daksha was beheaded (see previous two spreads), **Brahma** asked Shiva to bring Daksha back to life. But there was a problem. **Virabhadra** had cut off Daksha's head and thrown it into the sacrificial fire. So to make his return possible, Shiva arranged that he be given the head of one of the goats intended for the sacrifice. Goats, in Vedic symbology, represent entrapment in material nature. A goat's head seemed suitable for Daksha.

So when Daksha returned to the world of the living, he was physically transformed. This transformation had a profound effect on his consciousness, too. He found his heart, which had been polluted by envy, cleansed just as lake water is cleansed by autumn rains. Daksha was overcome with regret at what had happened; he realized he had been so blinded by jealousy that he had caused his own daughter to commit suicide. With tears in his eyes he apologized to Shiva: "I didn't recognize you for who you are. Instead, I threw the arrows of my sharp words at you in front of the assembly. You have corrected me as a father corrects a child. Please forgive my offense."

Satisfied with Daksha's repentance, Shiva pardoned him and then encouraged him to complete his sacrifice.

Daksha's name means "expert." As a progenitor, his role in the creation was to help populate the universe, and he is famous for his expertise in fathering many, many children. But a progenitor is also meant to protect the lives he gives. Daksha failed to protect his daughter because he couldn't tolerate the power and influence of the self-realized Shiva.

One of Daksha's other roles was to become expert at performing the ritualistic sacrifices that please the devas and thereby bring into the world all the things people desire. Shiva had renounced all material pleasures and absorbed himself in spiritual realization. Because spiritual realization is higher than the pursuit of base, temporary pleasure, Shiva was honored above Daksha for his achievements. This is why Daksha had been jealous of him. Daksha's envy so hardened his heart that he was able to stand by as his daughter burned to death before his eyes.

Here, Shiva stands above a humbled Daksha, who has pushed aside his raw grief to begin the process of rectifying the great wrongs he has committed.

The Eleven Rudras

Oil on canvas, 80 × 60 cm

The word *rudra* is cognate with the English words "red" and "ruddy," and the Rudras are identified in Vedic texts as eleven red-complexioned devas, intimately linked with **Shiva** and associated with the principle of destruction.

They are devas of space and time and represent the ten forms of life breath along with the intelligence. They live in the liminal space between consciousness and unconsciousness, between hard intelligence and the intuitive world of emotion. Rudra also means "howling." The eleven types of life breath cause everyone to howl when they abandon the mortal body, and that grief is felt most painfully halfway between the heart and the mind.

At the end of the last age in the cycle of four, Ananta Shesha, with whom the Rudras are also associated, begins the process of universal destruction by becoming slightly angry. A three-eyed Rudra then springs from between his eyebrows. He is known as Sankarshana, a form of Shiva, and like Shiva, he carries a trident.

In this painting we see a contemplative Shiva in the center shaking his *damaru* drum and holding in one of his hands the flame of destruction. He has begun his *tandava-nritya*, or dance of devastation. The Rudras, each wearing an expression of anger or pain, dance with him. As the universe is brought into existence by a song that causes the living beings and all atoms to dance into activity, and as the world's balance, rhythm, and harmony are maintained through the constant vibration of sound, so it is dissolved by a devastating song and dance. Shiva's rhythm breaks the bonds between atoms and returns all the material elements to their primordial state. Destruction of matter is a natural outcome of its creation, and Shiva's calm demeanor suggests that he understands his function simply as a cyclical necessity.

The Ganges Descends to Earth

Oil on canvas, 63 × 50 cm

By performing severe austerities, King Bhagiratha received a benediction from the celestial river Ganges that her waters, fully spiritual, would descend to earth for all to bathe in and become purified. But the river goddess Ganga was afraid that the force of her stream would bore through the earth and continue down to the lower, subterranean planets. King Bhagiratha assured her, "Like a cloth woven of threads extending as far as its length and breadth, this universe in all its latitude and longitude is under the power of **Vishnu. Shiva** is Vishnu's representative, and he can sustain your forceful waves on his head."

But despite his assurances, the king had not yet secured Shiva's cooperation, so he began to worship Shiva in order to win his favor. Shiva is easily pleased, and he soon smiled on the king. The king then asked him to carry the brunt of the Ganges's fall. Shiva acquiesced, and the Ganges began to flow from its origin in the spiritual world, through the planets of the devas, and down toward earth. The waters fell first on Shiva's head, and from there onto the Himalayas, and then down into the Indian lowlands.

The artist has painted the flowing water in a shimmer of light, suggesting the Ganges's spiritual origin. Shiva sits in meditation at the base of the stream in a Himalayan valley. In some depictions of this story, Shiva's matted hair is spread out in a net to catch the flow, but here he wears the traditional topknot of a yogi ascetic. The crescent moon, an attribute of Shiva, is just visible above his brow.

Ganesh

Pen and ink on paper, 76 × 41 cm

Ganesh is among the most popular devas. Son of **Shiva** and his wife Parvati, and loved throughout the Indian subcontinent and beyond, Ganesh, with his pot belly, elephant head, and ability to help his petitioners overcome obstacles, is known as the deva-guardian of thresholds and all other beginnings.

He has one tusk, symbolizing his ability to overcome duality. He broke off his second tusk to use as a pen while he wrote down the *Mahabharata.* His trunk is crooked to show the way around obstacles, and the Vedic swastika shows the right- and left-handed paths toward liberation. Like all the devas, he has a mount – in his case, a mouse, not shown in this drawing. Mice are masters of hiding and enjoying, unseen, the pleasures of others. In that sense, mice represent the soul, which hides behind illusion and yet takes for itself what is meant for God. Ganesh is master of the mouse, and guides these souls toward a more honest path.

As in this drawing, Ganesh is shown two-handed, with one hand raised in the *abhaya mudra*, signifying protection or refuge. In his other hand he holds a trident, signifying his mastery over past, present, and future. But often he is depicted holding a piece of candy, indicating his sweet nature and the rewards available to those who practice spiritual disciplines.

His enlarged abdomen reminds us that everything in life – both the good and the bad – are digestible by those who trust God's munificence.

Ganesh is often shown with two more hands, one holding an elephant goad and the other a noose. The first is used to prod humankind toward the path of devotion, and the second to capture material illusion and banish it from the mind. His elephant head symbolizes luck, strength, and powerful intellect.

Ganesh is famous for one pastime in particular: after compiling the Vedas and writing the *Srimad-Bhagavatam,* **Vyasa** wanted to record in poetry the history of the Pandavas and the Battle of Kurukshetra, but he needed a scribe. Ganesh's name was suggested. Ganesh, however, set a condition: he would write only as long as there was no break in the dictation.

But how could Vyasa dictate continually day and night? Agreeing to Ganesh's condition, Vyasa decided to make one of his own: Ganesh should not record anything without first having fully considered its meaning. This gave Ganesh pause in the dictation and Vyasa time to rest, and the *Mahabharata* was completed within three years.

The Prachetas

Oil on canvas, 120 × 90 cm

The Prachetas were ten brothers, princes, who, before their father considered them fit to rule, were sent to the seacoast to strengthen their character by practicing yoga and meditation. There they met **Shiva,** who taught them to recite the beautiful *Rudra-gita,* Shiva's personal hymn of praise to the Supreme, **Vishnu.** The Prachetas then entered the sea and performed their yoga underwater. After many, many years of chanting the *Rudra-gita* and becoming single-minded in their meditation, Vishnu appeared to them, accepted their devotion, and ordered them to return to rule their kingdom.

The Prachetas had been gone so long that their aging father had been unable to wait for their return. He had left his kingdom in the hands of his ministers so he could seek his own spiritual realization before he died. When the Prachetas emerged from the sea, they saw that the land and people had been neglected in their father's absence. The trees had grown tall and covered all the arable land. People were living in forests and appeared to have forgotten how to grow grains. The Prachetas knew that agriculture is essential for the advancement of civilization, and they decided to clear the land for crops.

At the time of universal devastation, Shiva emits fire and air from his mouth and burns the three worlds to ashes. Thinking their own thoughts of destruction, the Prachetas decided to follow their teacher and do the same. Here we see them beginning their work in a jungle of hugely overgrown trees.

Seeing that the Prachetas were burning all the trees to ashes, **Brahma,** whose duty it is to maintain harmony in the world, arrived to stop them. All of nature is under the care of various guardian spirits, and on Brahma's advice the lord of the trees offered his daughter in marriage to the Prachetas to pacify them.

This daughter was actually born of a sage and a heavenly nymph. After giving birth to the child, the nymph had abandoned her, but the moon deva had allowed the baby to suck nectar from his finger. The trees then cared for her, and after she married the Prachetas, she became the mother of **Daksha** during his second incarnation.

The Prachetas saw that the trees had grown tall and covered all the arable land.

shiva and mohini

Oil on canvas, 70 × 50 cm

Once, the devas and demons formed a truce to churn the milk ocean with the hopes of finding the elixir of immortality. Although time favored the demons' bid for power, the devas hoped the elixir would swing the balance back in their favor. But as soon as the elixir appeared, the demons snatched it for themselves. Because demons are dangerous to all beings, and immortal demons would be unstoppable, **Vishnu** agreed to help the devas regain the elixir. To do this, he took the form of a beautiful woman – Mohini – his only female avatar.

Mohini was so alluring that the demons couldn't resist her; she easily convinced them to turn the elixir over to her so she could distribute it on their behalf. But she gave it all to the devas.

The scene in this painting occurs later. Having heard the story of Mohini, and knowing she was actually Vishnu, **Shiva** became obsessed with the idea of seeing her. He went to Vishnu's abode, offered his worship, and then humbly asked if he could see Vishnu's Mohini form.

When Vishnu heard Shiva's request, he smiled gravely. Then he disappeared, and Shiva found himself in a spring forest. Suddenly, the most magnificent woman he had ever seen appeared. She was playing with a ball and flirting with him. Her hair had come loose from its braid, and she was twisting it around the fingers of her right hand. The soles of her soft feet were as red as coral, and her jeweled necklaces swayed as she bounced the ball. Shiva was so captivated that he forgot himself – as well as his wife and all the sages in attendance. Here we see him focused intently on a dancing Mohini, reaching for her hair to pull her toward him as she playfully eludes his grasp.

Sexual attraction is the basic principle of material existence, because the pursuit of intense physical pleasure makes one forget the soul's identity. Shiva is above this material pull, but Vishnu is Yogeshwara, the master of all mystics, and he captured Shiva through his Mohini form to make Shiva realize the power of his ability to create illusion.

While Lord Shiva observed the beautiful woman playing with the ball, she sometimes glanced at him and slightly smiled in bashfulness.

Srimad-Bhagavatam

shibi and the pigeon

Oil on canvas, 117 × 86 cm

Shibi is famous in ancient Indian history for his exemplary practice of a king's dharma and protecting all beings – human and animal – in his kingdom. When Shibi was told he could go to heaven after his death because of his selfless service and perfect execution of dharma, Shibi encouraged a good friend to go in his stead. His friend would not hear of it, and insisted that the worthy Shibi enjoy the fruits of his good qualities.

One tale of Shibi has lived on in the histories. It tells of the devas testing Shibi's tolerance. **Indra,** lord of heaven, took the form of an eagle, and Agni, the fire god, took the form of a pigeon. The eagle began to chase the poor pigeon, hoping to eat its flesh, but the would-be prey took shelter on the lap of compassionate King Shibi. The eagle insisted that Shibi give up the pigeon as its lawful prey. In response, Shibi offered to provide other food for the eagle.

But the eagle would settle for nothing short of the pigeon, so to protect this pigeon, who had accepted his shelter, King Shibi told the eagle it could eat as much of his body as equaled the weight of the pigeon. The eagle agreed, and Shibi began to cut off his flesh and weigh it on a scale. However, the pigeon, balancing on the other side of the scale, became heavier and heavier, and the king was forced to slice off more and more of his flesh. Finally, he realized he would have to give his whole body in place of the pigeon, for only this seemed to equal the pigeon's weight.

The devas were impressed with the king's willingness to sacrifice himself for a bird, and both Indra and Agni disclosed their identities to him, blessing him for his superlative compassion and restoring his body.

Here the artist has surrounded the scene with a tangle of trees. Trees are an ancient Vedic symbol of tolerance and humility. The leaves stand out a bright green, a color also reflected in Shibi's rich dress, reminding us of the vibrancy of life and the ultimate sacrifice Shibi was prepared to make for a small bird. It's interesting to note that Agni chose to take the form of a pigeon, which almost universally symbolizes the messenger between humans and the gods. But Vedic ideas take the symbol further: the pigeon also represents the human soul and its intrinsic spiritual nature. The crowned eagle, against which Shibi raises his arm, symbolizes arrogance – the sure destroyer of humility and the soul's ability to feel empathy for others.

Hamsa, the Swan Avatar

Oil on canvas, 70 × 43 cm

The four **Kumaras,** sons of **Brahma,** once asked their father about yoga, especially how practitioners can free themselves from material attraction and meditate on God. But Brahma didn't feel qualified to answer his sons' questions because his own mind was distracted from his yogic trance by the work of creation. Brahma then prayed to **Vishnu** to descend and teach the Kumaras – and through them, all those interested in self-realization through yoga.

Vishnu chose to descend in the form of a swan. When the Kumaras saw Hamsa, they humbly placed themselves behind their father while their father offered prayers. Then taking their cue from Brahma, they stepped forward and asked Hamsa their questions. Hamsa discussed the importance of meditation on Vishnu, the truth of the self, Vishnu's unique identity, and how all the yoga systems culminate in bhakti yoga, the yoga of devotion. He also discussed the virtues and pitfalls of yoga practice.

In this painting we see a four-headed Brahma standing with his hands folded in a universal gesture of respect, the four Kumaras on the lawn around him. Hamsa stands on a pillar, high above their heads, wearing a crown and shining with divine light. The crescent moon, symbolic of eternal life, gently illumines the sky. The artist has created a beautiful but mystical landscape to frame the figures. The rocky structure in the background, with its triangular shape crowned by a shrine, creates the subtle impression of a meditating yogi. Hamsa stands in front of the "yogi's" heart chakra to indicate the importance of the yoga of love.

One may wonder why Vishnu chose to appear in the form of a swan to discuss yoga. Swans are endowed with beauty and grace, but more importantly, they are said to have the capacity to separate milk from water – the essential from the nonessential – when the two have been mixed. Yoga is a vast topic, and much has been written about it; even if one has an aptitude for study, life is short. It takes many, many years to distill the substance from all the available knowledge about yoga. The swan represents the perfection of that endeavor.

Kalki and the End Times

Oil on canvas, 100 × 75 cm

When Kali-yuga, the current age of quarrel and hypocrisy, draws to a close about 427,000 years from now, Kalki will appear. An avatar of **Vishnu,** he is usually depicted riding the beautiful white horse Devadatta and killing all who remain in the world at that time.

The *Srimad-Bhagavatam* explains that by the end of Kali-yuga, people will be living in deplorable conditions. The sky will be dark, with the only light coming from the jewels on the heads of serpents. People will be forced to eat their children to survive. There will be years of excessive heat followed by years of excessive cold, and people will be unrestrained in their cruelty. The artist has reflected this idea in his background, where the sea rises over the cliffs, ready to crash down on the battlefield and wash everything clean.

An apocalyptic darkness pervades this work and serves as a foil to highlight Kalki, the emblem of all that is light and good. The only other light in this painting is the swath of blue sky, cutting a sharp diagonal through the ominous cloud cover and hinting that even as Kalki triumphs as the great leveler, the light of a new and better age is about to dawn. Those who are killed by Kalki's sword will be reborn in that new age, Satya-yuga, the age of righteousness that is the spring to Kali-yuga's winter.

Displaying his unequaled effulgence and riding with great speed, Kalki will kill by the millions those thieves who have dared dress as kings.

Srimad-Bhagavatam

The "Indweller" Revisited

Pastel on ingres paper, 60 × 45 cm

The **"Indweller,"** or Paramatma, is **Krishna** as witness and friend to all who live in material bodies. The Indweller lives in the "cave of the heart," and is sought after in meditation.

But he is only a partial expression of the Godhead. So here we will visit him again, because meeting him is, for many souls, the gateway to meeting him in his fullest expression in the form of beautiful, playful, and all-loving Krishna, the topic of the next section.

Meditation on God takes place in three stages in yoga practice. Think of it like the experience of approaching a mountain from a distance. As we walk toward the mountain, we see it shrouded in mist – we can tell it's tall and see its outline, but can't make out the details. This is similar to the understanding of God as a white light or a universally pervasive energy.

As we come closer, we begin to see the particulars of the mountain – the purple-gray of its rocks, the trees clinging to its sides, and the sheer magnificence of it as it rises above the surrounding landscape. This is the Paramatma, the Indweller, understanding of God. We have begun to see his qualities and characteristics, but we're still too far off to interact with the terrain.

Both of these perceptions of the mountain are different from what we can see and know about it when we're standing on its slopes.

How close to God are we willing to get? Is he that all-pervading, impersonal power like the mist-shrouded mountain? The divine oversoul like the purple-rocked mountain? A divine person with whom we can have an intimate relationship – the same mountain but met up close? God is, of course, one, and it's only our perception of him that varies.

So here we again meet the Indwelling Spirit and helper of the soul. He is characteristically blue, his gaze straight, equal. This is a clue to the Indweller's nature. He typically stands in the *samabhanga* pose, without bending, his limbs balanced perfectly against the vertical axis of his body. When the Indweller holds his head and body erect like this, he is showing himself to be in a state of equilibrium and tranquility. This is significant, because the Indweller is the impartial witness and support of the living beings' activities, and it's through his intimate knowledge of us that he knows just when to reveal the path leading higher up the mountain.

The Life of Krishna

Paintings of sacred Vrindavan can alter our view of reality. It's almost as if the world we look out at through our window has been painted in black-and-white stills, as if it were a faded memory of a time and place that is full of color and excitement, a world we have long forgotten. Vrindavan is that forgotten kingdom.

Krishna stands at the center of this kingdom. Along with Sri Radha and his family, neighbors, friends, cows, and all of nature, he makes the spiritual world glow with loving affection. He is the electricity that activates that world. That same electrical "Krishna-current" flows from the spiritual world to this world, infusing our mundane realm with vitality and flavor. For those who learn to perceive his energetic presence in *this* world, a new and vibrant understanding of reality beckons.

Doug Ball (Pariksit Dasa)
Govinda, 1975, oil on board, 35 × 26 cm

Krishna

Oil on canvas, 45 × 35 cm

The *Srimad-Bhagavatam* begins with obeisance to **Krishna:** "I meditate on Lord Krishna, the Absolute Truth and primeval cause of all causes of the creation, sustenance, and destruction of the manifested universes ..." A few verses later the text informs us that Krishna is the source of all manifestations of matter and spirit and all avatars of God.

Krishna is revealed in his most human aspect in the *Srimad-Bhagavatam's* Tenth Canto, especially the section describing his life in Vrindavan, a pastoral playground filled with forests and fields, cows and monkeys, and the ever-present sound of Krishna's flute.

Here we see Krishna lying back in the embrace of a tree's sprawling roots, his head pillowed by a mass of pink flowers. A blue lily decorates his ear, and his glowing yellow shawl seems to lift carelessly into the breeze. Cows, peacocks, and deer have come in pairs to hear his flute-song, and even the river joins in, lifting up on her watery fingers pink lotuses just beginning to open.

Krishna is the quintessential lover, and there is a romantic air to this painting as the tree above Krishna drips with honey-filled purple blossoms and the waterfall in the distance adds a soft percussion to the flute's soprano.

Real beauty is perceived by the soul's eye and not by the body's eye.

KEVIN YEE (RAMADASA ABHIRAMA DASA) 1980
MIRIAM BRIKS (DHRITI DEVI DASI)

Beautiful Krishna

Oil on canvas, 78 × 46 cm

Truth and beauty are interrelated, so it's no wonder that in **Krishna,** the Absolute Truth, we find the apex of all things beautiful. His lustrous body is the deep bluish-black of a fresh rain cloud during the rainy season. As rainfall glistens, so his body glistens, and his golden yellow *dhoti* is the color of a brilliant flash of lightning. He sits, his body gently curved, his head tilted to one side. A brightly-colored peacock feather dances on his turban, and around his neck hangs a garland of flowers. Lord Krishna's eyes, it is said, defeat the beauty of white lotuses, and his eyebrows move on his face like roving bees. As he places his charming bamboo flute to his lips and moves his fingers on it here and there, his face shines like the full autumn moon.

The Vedas describe Krishna's beauty as transcendent, otherworldly, and absolute. Such beauty stretches the limits of all possible experience and knowledge. How, then, can an artist possibly draw it, through pigments and brushes, onto canvas?

Yet artists try to do just that, both as an act of devotion and an act of compassion. As one nineteenth-century Bengali Vaishnava wrote, "If divine compassion, love, and justice can be portrayed by the pencil and expressed by the chisel, why can't the personal beauty of the deity, embracing all other attributes, be portrayed in poetry or picture or expressed by the chisel for the benefit of humankind? If words can impress thoughts, the watch indicate time, and signs tell us of history, why shouldn't the picture or sculpture evoke higher thoughts and feelings of the transcendental beauty of the divine person?"

People often ask why Krishna is blue. Indian aesthetes call "Krishna-blue" *shyam,* a color that speaks of beauty and love, youth and supreme attractiveness.

The Birth of Krishna

Oil on canvas, 90 × 60 cm

Krishna was born – that is, he appeared before his parents Vasudeva and Devaki – in a Mathura prison. Some texts describe the prison as a dungeon and others say his parents were under house arrest. All agree that Krishna was born in the dead of night. He appeared to them first in his awe-inspiring **Vishnu** form, carrying in his four hands his signature club, disc, lotus, and conch. Naturally, the appearance of God quelled their parental emotion. Overcome by reverence at seeing Vishnu before them, Vasudeva and Devaki composed themselves and offered heartfelt prayers to their divine son.

Despite knowing Krishna's actual identity as the supreme power in the universe, however, Vasudeva and Devaki were afraid for him. Six of their children had already been murdered by Devaki's cruel cousin, Kamsa, because of a prediction Kamsa had received that Devaki's eighth son would kill him. To save his life, Kamsa had smashed each of Devaki's newborn children on the prison's stone floor right before their mother's horrified eyes. To save this child, Devaki begged Krishna to hide himself. Although it is impossible to kill God, Krishna bowed to their love and agreed. After assuming his original two-armed form and appearing as a baby, Krishna told Vasudeva to take him to Nanda and Yashoda in Gokul.

Here we see Vasudeva carrying the child out of the prison. Krishna looks out at us and toward Vrindavan, where he will display his childhood pastimes with his most loving devotees.

It is dark midnight, and by Krishna's mystic potency, the locks have magically opened – note the open padlock on the prison door and the keys still hanging around one guard's neck. We see the curved *kukri* knife in the belt of the same guard, and his loose hold on the cheetah's chain. Both knife and cheetah indicate that these are fierce and loyal fighters, yet somehow they are asleep at their post. One cheetah yawns, offering no threat as Vasudeva, shielded by the divine Ananta Shesha, hurries past. The escape remains secret.

To the left of Vasudeva stands a sculpture of a crouching figure with a bowl of fire on his head. This image illustrates the Vedic concept of how everyone carries the burden of his or her karma until it burns out. The bell to the right represents the mind overcome by ignorance. It hangs unsounded by the guards, who are lost in a world of dreams and do not see either Vasudeva ("purity" or "goodness") or Krishna, reality in all its beauty and innocence.

The Butter Thief

Oil on canvas, 58 × 43 cm

One of the most famous scenes of Krishna's youth is his stealing of butter from the cowherd women (**gopis**) and feeding it to the monkeys. Here we catch him and his elder brother, **Balaram,** with his hand in a butter pot suspended from the ceiling while a *gopi* steps out for a minute. Krishna stole liberally from his own house, but he also went with his small friends to all the houses in his village to steal freshly-churned butter, yogurt, and sometimes milk.

Why steal butter? In her excellent book, *Windows Into the Infinite: A Guide to the Hindu Scriptures,* Barbara Powell offers this insight:

"The pots of butter represent the hearts of devotees. He breaks through the hard outer shell (ego, desire, ignorance, etc.) and releases the soft, sweet self within ... Krishna's breaking the pots corresponds to his breaking their hearts by prolonging the agony of the soul's yearning for him, and the ladies' anger reflects the frustration of the soul struggling for him. But like the butter inside which he devours, the women soften to him, are overcome with love for him, and surrender gladly to this love."

This painting is reminiscent of the Guler-Kangra style of miniature painting with its simple but elegant lines, limited palette, and focus on domestic elements. Even small details are carefully drawn. Here we see a smiling and peacock-feathered Krishna reaching into the butter pot a *gopi* has hung from a swing to protect it from the monkeys. The mother monkey, baby in tow, extends her hand, hoping Krishna will favor her. Balaram supports his brother on his shoulders and leans on his cowherd stick. Birds peck at seeds left in a bowl on the floor, and the butter churn stands to the left of the courtyard, obviously a much-used implement. The darker band at the top of the image as well as the two framing pillars close in the space; Krishna is literally stealing butter under this *gopi's* nose. This adds a delightful feeling of risk and naughtiness to the scene.

Krishna's fame as a butter thief is not reproachable, for by stealing butter he gave pleasure to his pure devotees.

Putana

Oil on canvas, 90 × 70 cm

After **Krishna's** appearance in the prison cell of Vasudeva and Devaki he was given to Nanda and Yashoda in Gokul to protect him from the cruel King Kamsa. Even so, because it had been predicted that our small hero would bring about the king's demise, Kamsa, eager to defeat the prediction, repeatedly sent demons and sorcerers to Gokul to kill Krishna.

Among the first to try was Putana, a child-eating witch who could change her form at will. Entering Krishna's cowherd village in the guise of a beautiful woman, she walked right into his private quarters without permission. Although there were many cowherd women present to protect the divine baby, no one thought to stop Putana, who looked like a goddess come to bless the child.

As she gazed on infant Krishna, she picked him up with apparent motherly tenderness and brought him to her breast. What the onlooking women didn't know was that she had smeared her nipples with a deadly poison. But baby Krishna knew, and knew too that he would have to kill her because of it. Putana laid him on her lap and opened her blouse. Krishna opened his mouth to accept her nipple, but with unrelenting force he suddenly grabbed hold of her breast with his small hands and proceeded to suck out not only the poison but the soul from her body.

Knowing her end was near and in excruciating pain, Putana began to sweat profusely and, flailing her arms like a speared octopus, begged Krishna to release her. Krishna, however, reciprocates the emotions of those who approach him, and because Putana had intended to take his life, he took hers. Still, she had approached him as a mother, so he awarded her soul liberation, allowing her to serve him as a wet nurse in the spiritual world.

As Putana died, she assumed her original, witch form, seen here, her body expanding to gigantic proportions. In this painting her frightened face resembles a Medusa, and her breasts like two hills with Krishna playing in the valley between them.

In the foreground we see a *gopi* in red, shocked at the scene before her. Other *gopis* look on from nearby. No one seems sure what to do. Infant Krishna, however, lifts a strand of Putana's hair as the witch dies, very much the way a victorious wrestler lifts an opponent's arm. Putana's own arms are reaching toward the ominously dark clouds, hinting at her inherent evil nature. In the distance, however, we see Gokul bathed in crepuscular rays from that same cloud bank, giving the town an appearance of spiritual purity and suggesting the final destination of Putana's soul.

Trinavarta

Oil on canvas, 80 × 60 cm

One day, while **Krishna** was a baby, his mother, Yashoda, was playing with him on her lap. Suddenly he became so heavy that she could no longer bear his weight. Confused, she sat him on the ground and began to pray to Narayana for his protection. Then, not knowing what else to do, she called over the brahmins, who tried to relieve the baby's mysterious problem by intoning mantras. Yashoda left Krishna sitting in her courtyard with the chanting brahmins while she tended to her household chores.

Meanwhile, Trinavarta, a demon in the form of a giant whirlwind, snatched Krishna away. Although little Krishna's weight was incalculable, Trinavarta easily lifted him and carried him miles above the simple homes of Vrindavan. The monstrous demon left a trail of clouds and smoke in his wake, and he vibrated a thunder that shook the cowherd villages below, drowning out the protective mantras the brahmins were now chanting in earnest.

For a few fateful minutes the entire pasturing ground for miles in every direction was overcast and filled with dust. Yashoda, covering her face to protect it from the harsh wind and blowing sands, ran frantically around the courtyard, looking for her beautiful boy.

When the tornado moved past her and the air calmed, Yashoda still could not find Krishna. She sat in the devastated pasture, crying piteously like a cow that has lost its calf.

But her baby was now miles above her and growing heavier by the moment. Krishna wrapped his small arms around Trinavarta's neck and let his weight choke the demon and force him down. Trinavarta landed on a stone slab in a field, his limbs dislocated and his spine smashed. Baby Krishna fell on top of him and was cushioned by the demon's body. Yashoda and the other cowherd women ran to pull him off the demon's broad chest, amazed at the miracle that had given him back to them after such a fall.

It's interesting to note how Trinavarta's cloak wraps almost protectively around Krishna. Although Krishna is in danger, he is aware of his supreme godhood and is not afraid. He looks like a child on a thrilling midway ride, and to enhance that impression the artist has not chosen dark, stormy colors for the ride in the sky but fresh blues and whites. The ominous colors are on the ground, where Krishna's mother has lost her son, but Krishna himself is having the time of his life.

Brahma's Maya Defeated

Oil on canvas, 54 × 40 cm

Just after **Krishna** killed a great python demon named Agha, he and his friends sat down to a forest picnic. As they were eating, the calves began to wander off in search of young grasses. Krishna didn't want to disturb his friends' lunch, so he went off himself to retrieve them.

Brahma had witnessed something miraculous during the powerful Agha's death: he had seen the brilliant light of Agha's soul leave Agha's body and merge with the body of Krishna. How could this small child have such power? Was this actually his worshipful deity, the Supreme Godhead? But how could his Lord be a little boy who, like any small village boy, liked to play with his friends?

Brahma decided to test Krishna's power and display a little of his own. He took the calves and cowherd boys, induced in them a mystic slumber, and hid them in a cave. What would Krishna do when he returned to find both boys and calves gone?

But Krishna is omniscient. Aware of Brahma's trick he simply expanded himself as the missing cowherd boys and calves and went on with his day as if nothing had happened. Brahma was confused to see them. He returned to the cave; the boys and calves he had taken were still there. Where did these others come from?

A year later – only a moment of Brahma's time – Brahma returned the original cowherd boys and calves. Krishna then revealed to him how he had expanded himself to take their places. This painting depicts the moment immediately after Brahma understands he's been tricked. Here he kneels submissively before a young Krishna and cries tears of joy. Krishna stands opposite him, a lump of food in his left hand and a look of tolerance on his face. While he appreciates Brahma's apology, he is eager to get back to playing with his friends, whom he has missed for an entire year.

In the background the artist has added another dimension of Vrindavan – a stag and tiger lay together on the grass. In Vrindavan there is no envy or malice, because all beings find their pleasure only in pleasing the center of their existence, Sri Krishna.

How could this small child have such power? Was this actually his worshipful deity, the Supreme Godhead?

Krishna Greets His Parents

Oil on canvas, 210 × 305 cm

When **Krishna** and **Balaram** return from the pastures in the late afternoons, their parents wait for them with open arms. Yashoda is especially anxious to see the boys come home. Balaram, who is a little older, might continue to play with some friends, as seen here (he is wearing the blue turban), but Krishna always runs into his mother's arms. Later, she and the young **gopis** in the painting will offer Krishna and Balaram a well-prepared meal – the boys are famished when they return from cowherding.

Of course, what Krishna and Balaram really hunger for is the love of their devotees. The loving environment of Vrindavan, in fact, is perfectly constructed for affectionate exchanges, and this is why Krishna so relishes the mood of the devotees who live there. The setting is also ideal, with its mixture of family, friends, and the earth's natural creatures – cows, birds (in this painting we can see a peacock on the roof in the background and a dove descending from the trees), and plants of all varieties. Every relationship that exists in Vrindavan is lived to perfection, each centered on Krishna, the absolute and most darling recipient of love.

The artist has focused much of the mood of this painting in the eyes of the persons it depicts. Krishna and Yashoda look at one another with unrestrained affection and joy. In Nanda's eyes we also see a father's pride. A cowherd boy looks at Krishna from the side, perhaps waiting for the moment when Krishna will resume their interrupted game. And the young cowherd girls on the steps portray a mixture of eagerness and shyness, their eyes full of laughter and play.

Every relationship that exists in Vrindavan is lived to perfection, each centered on Krishna.

In Kaliya serpent's coils

Oil on canvas, 90 × 60 cm

A small section of the **Yamuna** River, where **Krishna** played and bathed with his many cowherd friends, flowed off into a lake that was the home of a many-hooded serpent named Kaliya. The serpent's fiery poison boiled the lake's waters, making it off limits to the people of Vrindavan. The vapors were so poisonous that birds overhead would fall dead into the lake, and whenever the breeze carried the fumes to shore, the nearby creatures and vegetation would shrivel up and die.

Unable to tolerate Kaliya's pollution of the Yamuna, Krishna climbed a nearby kadamba tree, ready to jump into the roiling waters and battle the powerful serpent. After all, Krishna appeared in this world to purify it by subduing all demoniac elements, and Kaliya represented the darkest of the world's polluters.

Krishna tightened his belt and plunged in, frolicking in Kaliya's watery domain like an elephant bathing. Hearing the commotion, Kaliya was incensed: "Who," he wondered, "would have the temerity to trespass in my waters?" When he saw Krishna, as beautiful as a lotus flower, his venom increased a thousandfold, and he wrapped Krishna in his many coils and bit him on the chest. The cowherds watching from the bank, who loved Krishna more than life itself, nearly fainted.

Seeing his friends' fear, Krishna decided to get down to business. He freed himself from Kaliya's grip and began to dance on the demon's many hoods, as we see here. When one head would not submit, he kicked down on that one harder than the others, until gradually each head was kicked into obeisance. This graceful dance was viewed by the devas, who came from the higher planets to provide the music for Krishna's dance. Soon, Kaliya's many wives appeared on the scene to beg mercy for their husband. Krishna spared Kaliya, but ordered him to leave the Yamuna forever.

The Kaliya story is a frequently painted pastime. In this version, the artist has used highly saturated colors against a smoggy sky to accentuate the damage Kaliya has done to beautiful Vrindavan. Krishna looks down almost demurely as he dances, stepping from hood to hood, with his flute tucked in his belt. Spots of pink decorate his cheeks, hinting at his exertion. With his left hand he grasps one of Kaliya's thrashing tails, suggesting that the work of subduing Kaliya does not require his stronger right hand, and a gentle smile plays on his lips. Kaliya has not yet surrendered – his fangs still drip venom – and he glistens with a black evil as he arches forward to continue his attack.

The Lifter of Govardhana

Oil on canvas, 90 × 130 cm

The Vedas teach that humans and devas are interdependent: humans perform sacrifices and offer the devas their share, and the devas, as controllers of natural forces, in turn supply humans with whatever help nature needs to provide to make their lives comfortable. Those who enjoy the devas' gifts without acknowledging their benefactors are actually considered thieves.

Directly or indirectly, all humans and animals live on food grains, and grains require rainfall. Rainfall is a result of sacrifice – part of the pact between humans and devas. So when **Indra,** the deva in charge of rain, saw **Krishna** discourage Vrindavan's cowherds from offering him his yearly sacrifice, he was outraged and decided to teach the cowherds a lesson, using rain as a weapon.

Soon black clouds rolled in over Vrindavan, accompanied by high winds, thunder, lightning, and hail mixed with sheeting rain. Humans, animals, and all the food grasses were hammered by the cold deluge of Indra's anger.

With nowhere else to turn, the cowherds begged Krishna for help. To save them, Krishna lifted Govardhana Hill as an umbrella. He then called to his relatives and neighbors to come in out of the rain.

Krishna held the hill for seven days, and life went on so naturally that no one felt any disturbance from Indra's storm.

Krishna's parents stand just under Krishna to his left. Yashoda worries the hill's weight will be too much for her tender son to bear. Nanda holds his cowherding stick at the ready. If Krishna falters, he will quickly reach up and catch the weight of the hill on his stick.

One young boy has brought Krishna a garland. **Balaram,** his plow on his shoulder, speaks to someone with pride. Behind him, two cowherd men appear to be conjecturing about how such a young boy could pick up a hill. And behind them, a turbaned cowherd man looks to his neighbor with pleasure; his neighbor seems equally pleased. The pure white cows, their ornate blankets not even dampened by Indra's storm, look up in adoration, while Indra's lightning strikes impotently in the background.

"O residents of Vraja, if you wish you may now come under this hill with your cows."

Krishna Kills the Demon Keshi

Oil on canvas, 53 × 40 cm

Having been instructed by Kamsa to do away with **Krishna,** the demon Keshi took the form of a giant and ferocious horse. On entering the precincts of Vrindavan, Keshi tore up the earth with his hooves and scattered the clouds with his mane. His whinnying terrified the deer and other forest creatures. Krishna understood Keshi's challenge and accepted it.

The horse-demon charged, roaring like a lion, his jaws open so wide that he looked as though he could swallow the sky. Keshi then reared up on his two back legs to thrash Krishna with his stonelike hooves. But to his surprise Krishna grabbed him by his legs and twirled him around like a weightless puppet. Finally letting go of the horse, the now unconscious Keshi flew one hundred bow-lengths before landing.

When Keshi regained consciousness, he again charged Krishna with his mouth open. Krishna laughed to see the horse's open mouth. He held up his thumb and said, "Are you looking for something to eat? Try this!" And his left fist went down Keshi's throat like a snake entering a hole. Krishna then expanded his arm and allowed it to become extremely hot. His armed filled the demon's throat and suffocated him, proving once again the foolishness of challenging Krishna or siding with the universe's evil forces.

One can sense Keshi's muscular energy beneath his shiny coat. The artist has deliberately painted this piece with a low horizon, forcing the viewer to look up at Keshi with the luminous Krishna. The dust in the atmosphere and the dark clouds overhead blur and soften the town of Vrindavan in the background and give it a purplish cast. This allows Vrindavan and its residents to recede safely into the distance while Krishna deals with this latest challenge to his supremacy.

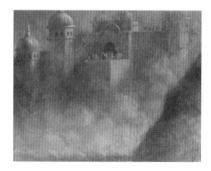

Keshi tore up the earth with his hooves and scattered the clouds with his mane.

KEVIN YEE (RAMADASA ABHIRAMA DASA)   1984
MIRIAM BRIKS (DHRITI DEVI DASI)

Radha and Krishna

Oil on canvas, 56 × 72 cm

People often ask, "Who is that girl with **Krishna?**" She is **Radha,** his other half, his shakti, and his greatest devotee.

Radha and Krishna together remind us that God is both the served and the servant, the beloved and the lover. In the *Gita,* Krishna says of himself that he is the source of all that is good and powerful and beautiful in this world – the original seed of existence, the heat in fire, the life of all that is alive, the intelligence of the intelligent, the strength of the strong, the vastness of the ocean, the immovability of the Himalayas. As the best essence of all things, who can worship him better than he can worship himself? Therefore Krishna manifests as Radha, the ideal worshiper and the mother of compassion. As Radha, he is God the worshiper, and as Krishna he is God the worshipped.

The *maha-mantra* (Hare Krishna, Hare Krishna, Krishna Krishna, Hare Hare/ Hare Rama, Hare Rama, Rama Rama, Hare Hare), which according to the Vaishnava tradition includes all other prayers, is aimed at both Radha and Krishna. Hare is the vocative form of Hara (a name for Radha), and by reciting her name we beseech her to let us serve Krishna.

Here Krishna sits with Radha on a flower-wrapped swing in the holy land of Vrindavan.

They are the epitome of young romantic lovers, but lovers in the spiritual sense, free from selfish demands and interested only in serving each other. As Krishna is both worshipped and worshiper, so in the land of Vrindavan worship and selfless service are nondifferent.

Doug Ball (Pariksit Dasa)
Radha and Krishna Swinging
1979, oil on canvas, 52 × 40 cm

Radha and Lalita

Oil on canvas, 77 × 63 cm

As **Radha** is **Krishna's** feminine counterpart, so the **gopis** are counterparts of Radha, each expressing a facet of Radha's love for Krishna. Here we see Lalita, Radha's best friend and confidante.

Young love is spicier when it's shared with friends, and Lalita adds to Radha's and Krishna's loving banter her particular flavors of diplomacy, wit, sprightly humor, and the kind of wise advice only a best girlfriend can give.

In this painting, both girls are about fifteen. In young adolescence, love is still simple and innocent, yet full of drama, and young lovers spend most of their time picking quarrels and making peace, contriving to meet one another and pining away when a tryst is impossible. Here, Radha holds a bouquet of peacock feathers, signifying that Krishna is elsewhere. She misses him intensely. Lalita whispers soft, consoling words into Radha's ear, perhaps suggesting they crush some of the roses we see in the background into ink so they can write Krishna a letter.

Spiritual love has many moods, but the most intense ecstasy is felt when there is separation between lover and beloved. When we're in love, everything we see reminds us of our beloved. If that love is as all-consuming as Radha's is for Krishna (and his for her), a feeling of oneness between the two lovers develops that can be discerned even in external ways. Radha, thinking of Krishna's sapphire complexion, likes to wrap herself, as here, in blue, and Lalita, who has given her life to serve her friend, herself wears a sari the color of peacock feathers to always remind Radha of her lover.

Spiritual love has many moods, but the most intense ecstasy is felt when there is separation between lover and beloved.

Krishna's Flute calls the Gopis

Oil on canvas, 60 × 90 cm

This painting depicts a full-moon evening in autumn. **Krishna,** standing to the left under an inviting archway of trees, plays his flute to invite the **gopis,** the young cowherd women of Vrindavan, to his *rasa* dance. His beautiful body is curved in three places. With his yellow garments and garland of forest flowers, he makes an enchanting Cupid.

The *gopis* hear Krishna's flute-song and feel its lure. They have as much power to resist him as leaves can resist an autumn breeze. The forest is fragrant with flowers, the night cooling and festive, and the *gopis* will soon rush into Krishna's all-loving company. Their attraction to the flute-song has been increased by the rising full moon, the red horizon, the cool atmosphere, and the blossoming flowers.

It's as if they are already dancing. One *gopi,* her head turning, drops a clay pot the moment the flute-song enters her ears, while another *gopi* abandons her cooking. We get a glimpse of the forgotten husbands and children running out to catch their wives and mothers before they are gone.

The full moon has risen – we can just see it through the branches of the trees in the foreground of the painting. The trees themselves are entwined like lovers. A single moonbeam, an emissary of the flute-song, bathes one special *gopi,* who reaches upward with ardent attention. This is **Sri Radha,** Krishna's eternal consort. The flute-call is especially meant for her.

The artist has subtly indicated an important theme relating to the *rasa* dance. Although all the *gopis* are from the same village and know one another, they each hear the message of Krishna's flute as intended for themselves alone. The artist has used moonlight to make sure we can distinguish each *gopi,* but also glazes with an overall rosy hue to diffuse, soften, and finally harmonize them as they rush out to meet the beloved of all their hearts. The *rasa* dance is a group dance, and while Krishna calls each *gopi* individually, they must become one in spirit to join him in this pastime.

The flute-song seen metaphorically represents the call to the soul to shed all worldly identification and return to its own essence as a lover of Krishna, reservoir of all love. The *gopis'* response to the flute teaches us the total abandon and single-minded devotion required to hear the call and answer it.

KEVIN YEE (RAMADASA ABHIRAMA DASA)
MIRIAM BRIKS (DHRITI DEVI DASI)

Young Love

Oil on canvas, 70 × 55 cm

What's the difference between the mundane and spiritual worlds? The material world is only a reflection of complete reality, like the reflection of a tree in water or our face in a mirror. Absorbed in self-interest we embrace **Krishna's** creation but lose sight of Krishna himself. As a result, what is spiritual becomes distorted, tainted, colored by prejudice.

The material world is all about exploitation. We work hard to enjoy ourselves here, but are forced to succeed always at another's expense. We can't help it; it's how the world works. We can't even keep fed or warm or sheltered without stealing the life or home of some other being.

But if we are fortunate to be reminded of our spiritual roots, we can start to see things differently. When material self-interest shifts to spiritual self-interest, we then find ourselves on the doorstep of the spiritual world, a world not of exploitation but of love and service.

Stepping up to the threshold we meet the **Indweller,** who guides us across the threshold to where we will have the opportunity to gradually overcome fear of God and seek a deeper intimacy with him. If we are brave enough to live up to our fullest potential, we may even find ourselves in Vrindavan, where Krishna expresses himself most completely and where you'll always find him with his beloved **Radha.**

Radha and Krishna are eternally youthful and eternally in love, and they display this love most openly in Vrindavan. They show us that a relationship with God is not static or one way – petitioner to Supreme – but an endless reciprocation of mutual love and service.

In this painting the artists have captured a little of the sweetness of this reciprocation. Caught in their glance is a transcendental dynamic by which Krishna looks at Radha and becomes more beautiful in his happiness. Radha, seeing she has pleased Krishna, feels such joy that her own beauty increases. When Krishna sees his glowing Radha, his own beauty and sweetness blossom. And so it continues without limit.

One who is attracted by the beauty of Radha and Krishna cannot be attracted by the false beauty of this material world.

motherly Love

Oil on canvas, 148 × 170 cm

Rasa is a Sanskrit term specific to **Krishna** bhakti traditions. It refers to the emotional voice of a soul's relationship with God in devotion and God's reciprocation with that love. Love for God can be expressed through any of the relationships we use to express love in our human lives – between lover and beloved, friend and friend, master and servant, and parent and child. Although Krishna can never be less than supreme, he is a connoisseur of *rasa*. If a soul's *rasa* is to love and care for him as a child, he willingly becomes a child for that soul, playing the part so perfectly that the soul is lost in a rapture of affection.

Here we see a young Krishna surrounded by his mother, Yashoda (in white), and other women immersed in the *rasa* of motherhood. Yashoda thinks of Krishna with such deep maternal affection that she sometimes disciplines him, determined, like any mother, to make sure her son grows up moral and responsible. And even when Krishna does impossible things like lift the **Govardhana** Mountain, Yashoda's simple love is not disturbed. Instead of awestruck by the fact that her son is holding up a mountain, she stands next to him with a plate of fruits and candies, worrying, again like any mother, that her child is too thin.

This painting depicts a late-afternoon exchange between Yashoda and her helpers and child Krishna. Every afternoon, when Krishna returns home from herding the cows with his friends, his mother and her assistants gently remove his ornaments and bathe and dress him for dinner. To the left we see a basket of ornaments. His mother holds his hand in hers as if she has just removed his jeweled bangle. His ankle bells and necklaces have already been removed, and his headdress is now a simple flower wreath. Krishna's eyes are closed, as if, like any little boy, he is sleepy after a long day of play.

> **"My dear son, because of playing all day, your body has become covered with dust and sand. Therefore, come back, take your bath and cleanse yourself."**

Sri Radha

Oil on canvas, 52 × 42 cm

As **Krishna** is the source of all avatars of God, so his consort **Sri Radha** is the source of all shaktis. Radha is the original goddess and the original form of spiritual energy – she is God in the form of his pure love energy.

In bhakti literature, Krishna is compared to the sun and Radha to the sunshine. Both exist simultaneously, but one comes from the other. Still, we can't quite say that the sun exists before the sunshine, because as soon as there is sun, there is sunshine. More importantly, the sun has no meaning without sunshine. But neither could sunshine exist without the sun. Sun and sunshine coexist, each essential to the existence of the other.

So it may be said that the sun and the sunshine are simultaneously one and different. Likewise, Radha and Krishna are inconceivably one and different. They are in essence a single entity who manifests as two distinct individuals in order to share love. As the bhakti tradition teaches: "Lord Krishna enchants the world, but Sri Radha enchants him." Sri Radha is the full power, and Lord Krishna is the possessor of that full power. The two are not different, just as musk and its scent are inseparable. And yet they have taken two forms to enjoy a relationship.

Here we see Radha pining for Krishna in the madness of deep love. In the background we see **Uddhava,** Krishna's emissary and look-alike, reading the **gopis** a letter Krishna has sent them to ease the pain they feel at his absence. All the *gopis* listen avidly, but Radha instead focuses on a bumblebee resting on a rose.

The artist has chosen to decorate the area around Radha with pink wild roses, an ancient symbol of secret first love. The bumblebee, called *madhu* (honey or sweetness) in Sanskrit and itself a symbol of love – in bhakti texts, Cupid's bowstring is said to be composed of humming bees – wears the dark stripes that remind Radha of her beloved. Radha accepts the bumblebee as Krishna's real emissary and asks it about Krishna's whereabouts.

Radha and Krishna are in essence a single entity who manifests as two distinct individuals in order to share love.

A Meditation

Oil on canvas, 130 × 120 cm

Along the banks of the **Yamuna** River, the Vrindavan forests are thick with flowering vines. Green parakeets flit from tree to tree as a soft breeze from the Malaya hills stirs swarms of bumblebees to search for honey. The full glowing moon of spring distributes its cooling rays out of love for **Krishna,** and at just such a time Krishna begins the *rasa* dance by inviting the **gopis** with his flute-song.

Gopis rush to join the dance, and **Radha,** their queen, sings beautiful songs to enchant Krishna's mind. Suddenly, Radha disappears, and the *rasa* dance comes to a halt. The flute-song calls Radha's name out into the night as Krishna goes to search for his beloved.

In this painting, he has just found her hiding in a secluded grove. Krishna is lord of the Moon Dynasty, and the unbroken disk of the full moon glows red – a lamp to help him find his Radha. Night-blooming lotuses open at his feet. Krishna is the springtime of Radha's life, but Radha sometimes flavors her love for him with sulking, as depicted here. Krishna will play a sweet melody to draw her out, and here he raises his flute to his lips to charm her.

Poets write that Radha wears "a silken sari of modesty," and on Her forehead "a red dot of loveliness." Her body is perfumed with musk, and she wears a necklace "adorned with jewels made of ecstasy."

Everything about Radha, from how she stands to what she wears, indicates something about her special love for Krishna. That she braids and ornaments her hair in a particular way symbolizes her hidden emotions of love for him. Her black eyeliner indicates her cleverness in how she attracts Krishna. Her forest-flower garland represents her personal qualities, and the blue of her sari her unending remembrance of her Lord.

sudama and κrishna

Oil on canvas, 110 × 80 cm

Krishna had a dear school friend named Sudama. Sudama was a poor brahmin who, with his wife, lived simply, barely keeping body and soul together. They were nonetheless peaceful, because they had transcended material urges through their spiritual knowledge. Sudama was particularly learned in the Vedas, and he knew that his friend Krishna was actually his worshipable Lord. So he and his wife spent their lives in meditation on his friend and cared for little else.

Sudama's wife, however, did have one other concern, and that was for her husband's frail health. One day she broached a delicate subject: "Lord Krishna is your personal friend, and you are his dear devotee. I cannot see you wanting for food. Please go to him. Without your even asking I'm sure he'll give you whatever you need because it's his nature to be merciful."

Sudama was reluctant to go to his friend with his needs, but after his wife repeatedly begged him he finally agreed. "After all," he reasoned, "at least I'll have the opportunity to see Krishna's beautiful face once again."

Before leaving for Krishna's palace in Dwaraka, Sudama asked his wife for a gift to give to Krishna, for he knew it would be disrespectful to arrive empty-handed. His wife gave him everything they had: four handfuls of broken rice.

When Sudama arrived in Dwaraka he was startled by the enthusiasm of Krishna's reception. Before Sudama even had a chance to pay his own respects, Krishna embraced him. He then offered Sudama a seat and had fruit and a drink brought. **Rukmini,** Krishna's principal queen, fanned Sudama with a whisk to make sure he was comfortable. Here we see her assisting Krishna in bathing Sudama's feet. This was for Krishna an ultimate act of humility and affection, and we can see a tear sparkling in his eye as he pours water from a conch.

The artist has used a traditional symbol of Krishna bhakti on the palace walls – the lotus. The lotus is one of the usual eight auspicious symbols incorporated into classical bhakti art. It is the symbol of plenty and creativity, and is associated with **Lakshmi,** the goddess of fortune, of whom Rukmini, shown holding the water pot, is an avatar. Vaishnava poets also refer to Krishna's feet as "lotus feet" to capture their softness, and his eyes as *kamalaksha,* "lotus eyes," to capture their romantic beauty.

shishupal Beheaded

Oil on canvas, 147 × 196 cm

Vedic peoples performed elaborate sacrifices, like the emperor's Rajasuya, shown here, to honor **Vishnu.** Yudhishthira, eldest of the Pandava brothers, presided at one of history's largest Rajasuyas. It was attended by devas, kings, and numerous brahmins and sages, and even by **Krishna** himself.

As was customary, one person at the sacrifice would be chosen to receive the first worship. All but Shishupal, a demon king, chose Krishna.

From childhood Shishupal had inexplicably hated Krishna. Naturally, then, when he witnessed the affection, prayers, and general glorification aimed at Krishna at the beginning of the sacrifice, he could barely stomach it. He leaped from his seat and spat venomous insults. The great kings drew their swords.

But Krishna would not allow a fight to erupt in the middle of a sacred rite. He called for his sharp disc weapon and flung it at the demon, severing Shishupal's head as easily as one slices a banana. Shishupal's soul then merged with Krishna's body in front of the entire assembly.

Here we see an incensed **Arjuna** (with bow) and Bhima (with club) marching forward to attack Shishupal. Yudhishthira stands regally to Krishna's right, and we can just see Parashuram, an ax-wielding sage, standing a little distance to the left.

All the light in the painting flows between a golden-dressed Krishna and Shishupal, who wears a rich, red garment, suggesting the passion and violence in his nature. The interior of the room is otherwise dark and the draperies and garments of the other participants muted to keep the eye focused on the main players in this drama. This darkness is broken only by the backlighting of an almost watercolored sky against a hazy, white palace. The insubstantiality of the palace, when contrasted with the sharp details of the scene, suggests that life and death are being played out right in this room; the viewer need not look beyond to find them. As did the Romantic artists who inspired him, this painter has used a darkened interior against a brilliantly-hued exterior to symbolize human existence standing between the temporal and the eternal – certainly a theme of this story.

The painter has chosen a horizontal format and given us a spectator's view, which helps emphasize the movement of the disc. Shishupal, grimacing in anger and surprise, is thrown back, although a solid wall of Krishna's supporters, pillars, and draperies seems to block just how far he can fall.

Balaram Drags Hastinapur

Oil on canvas, 61 × 46 cm

Duryodhana, the eldest of the Kuru princes, had a beautiful daughter named Lakshmana. Warrior girls often chose their husbands by setting tests of valor, and when Lakshmana was of marriageable age, Duryodhana arranged a tournament and invited many princes to try to win her hand.

Just as Lakshmana was about to present her chosen prince the victory garland, **Krishna's** son, Samba, arrived. Seeing Lakshmana's extraordinary beauty, Samba simply lifted her onto his chariot and began to drive away. This was almost expected behavior at these events; if a young "kidnapper" showed his prowess and defended himself well against the girl's pursuing relatives, the girl would welcome the marriage, and both families would embrace the union.

When the Kurus saw Lakshmana being spirited away by the brave Samba, they dispatched six of their most experienced warriors to arrest the culprit. Samba fought like a lion, but in the end he was overpowered. Although Samba's courage and skill had not gone unnoticed by the Kuru elders or his new bride, the Kurus decided to arrest him to assert their own prowess and destroy the pride of Samba's clan.

Narada, witness to the fight, went immediately to Samba's family and told them about the unfair battle. **Balaram,** elder brother of Krishna and shown here in blue, assured them he would sort things out. Duryodhana, after all, had been his student.

At first, the Kurus were pleased to see Balaram, but when he demanded they bring Samba and his new wife out to him, they insulted his family and especially his beloved younger brother, Krishna.

Balaram could not tolerate the Kurus' pride. How could they belittle Krishna when even the devas worship him? Balaram thought them drunk with power and decided to rid the earth of them.

Taking his plow, Balaram struck the earth with such force that he created a fault line along the city border. He then began to drag the city toward the nearby **Ganges** River. A great tremor passed through the city. Seeing their city tumbling about like a raft at sea, the Kurus became terrified, and to save their lives they brought Samba and Lakshmana out of the city and surrendered to Balaram.

Yamuna Prays to Balaram

Oil on canvas, 110 × 70 cm

Once, when Balaram, **Krishna's** elder brother, was living in Dwaraka, he returned to Vrindavan for a two-month visit. It had been some years since his foster parents, Nanda and Yashoda, had seen him, and they missed him intensely. His village friends had also missed him, as did the **gopis** he loved.

After spending time pacifying his parents and friends, Balaram decided to go with his *gopis* to a garden on the bank of the Yamuna River and to perform a *rasa* dance. The garden was bathed in the rays of the full moon and caressed by breezes bearing the fragrance of night-blooming lotuses. As the night grew late Balaram felt beads of perspiration blossom like snowflakes on his face and saw that his *gopis* were similarly tired. Thinking to relieve everyone's fatigue by playing in the Yamuna's waters, he asked the river to come to him.

The river goddess, however, decided that Balaram was inebriated – he and the *gopis* had been drinking a honey wine they found flowing from a tree hollow, making the entire forest even more fragrant – so she hesitated to heed his call. But she was mistaken; Balaram was not intoxicated with wine but with joy.

Balaram then grabbed his plow. "Disrespecting me," he said to the river, "you do not come when I call you but rather move only by your own whim. Therefore with the tip of my plow I shall bring you here in a hundred streams!" Even today one can see the many channels created by Balaram's plow.

Yamuna, trembling, quickly approached Balaram and folded her hands in prayer. Here we see the personified Yamuna, dressed in a watery veil, offering her prayers to a milk-white Balaram. He looks on with compassion as she stands amid the white lotus flowers rising from the river bottom. White flowers also speckle the forest floor around Balaram's feet. White is the color of purity and transcendence and of the pacification of one's lower drives, and the artist's choice of white in both the foreground and the background suggests the undercurrents of spiritual meaning that flow through this pastime.

Balaram will go on to play in the Yamuna's waters, and when he is finished, she will offer him a garland of unfading lotuses and garments as blue as the ocean.

The Kidnapping of Rukmini

Oil on canvas, 31 × 41 cm

Rukmini, daughter of Bhishmaka, was renowned for her beauty and royal qualities. She was aware of **Krishna's** beauty and qualities too, and resolved that he would make an ideal husband for her. Krishna also wanted to marry her. But there was one obstacle: her brother envied Krishna's charm and power and forbade his sister to marry him. Instead, he wanted her to marry his friend **Shishupal,** an avowed enemy of Krishna, whom Krishna eventually beheaded.

Rukmini was a dutiful sister, and she outwardly agreed to her brother's proposal. Still, she could not bear to see herself married to the offensive Shishupal. On the eve of her marriage, therefore, she wrote Krishna a letter begging him to kidnap her before her marriage. She sent this letter with a brahmin messenger to Dwaraka, where Krishna lived.

On receiving her letter Krishna did not waste a moment. He mounted his chariot and flew like the wind to rescue Rukmini before she was forced to go through with the wedding. When he arrived and caught a glimpse of her in the midst of her relatives, he saw his **Lakshmi,** the goddess of fortune (of whom she is an avatar).

In this romantic scene, Krishna has claimed his bride with heroic strength and dramatic flair. Arrows fly overhead as the two gaze into one another's eyes for the first time – the true moment of marriage. Above them the sky reflects both blues and golds, suggesting that the universe is in harmony with this union.

> **"O beauty of the worlds, having heard of your qualities, which enter the ears of those who hear and remove their bodily distress, and having also heard of your beauty, which fulfills all the visual desires of those who see, I have fixed my shameless mind upon you, O Krishna."**
>
> **From Rukmini's letter to Krishna**

Krishna Teases Rukmini

Oil on canvas, 130 × 90 cm

The scene in this painting is many years into **Krishna** and **Rukmini's** marriage – at a time when they have already raised their eleven children. It's early evening, and the moon is just beginning to rise. Smoke from the incense burning in the room wafts lazily through the lattice, and the air outside is fragrant with *cameli* flowers. Krishna is relaxing on a seat, two maidservants at his feet. Rukmini has just taken the yak-tail fan from one of these women – it's milky white in her hand – and begun to fan her husband, her ankle bells tinkling softly between the pleats of her sari as she moves.

By this time Krishna has married many queens, but Rukmini has never lost her simple affection for him. Still, a woman's beauty is more pronounced when she is angry, so Krishna decides to grind her heart with the pestle of his words.

He calls her "princess" to remind her that before their marriage she had many royal suitors. Her parents had even sanctioned her marriage to someone else. Why had she chosen Krishna, who was not her equal in wealth or status? Rukmini had claim to her father's large kingdom, whereas Krishna's father had been imprisoned when Krishna was a child and had lost all his property. Krishna went on to describe his many apparent disqualifications, and finally he suggested that Rukmini divorce him and marry someone more suitable.

Krishna was joking, of course, but Rukmini did not take his words in that spirit. She was fully in love with her husband, whom she knew to be the master of the three worlds. He had never spoken such harsh words to her, and they confused her. Was Krishna, who is transcendental to everything in this world, renouncing her? She knew she could not live without him. Her heart began to pound and her throat closed. She lowered her head. Then, as the thought of losing Krishna gripped her mind, she dropped the yak-tail fan and fainted, her beautiful hair scattering as she fell.

Krishna was immediately contrite. He rose from his seat and, taking Rukmini on his lap, placed his cooling hands on her face. He then embraced her and said, "I wanted to irritate you, and I was expecting you to counter my joking words. But you took them seriously. I'm sorry. O perfection of love, I was simply trying to enjoy your beautiful face when it was angry. But your love is so deep and humble that I have no way to repay your devotion."

JUDY KOSLOFSKY (JADURANI DEVI DASI)   1980

The surrender of Draupadi

Oil on canvas, 68 × 50 cm

Draupadi, the fire-born, was married to the five Pandava brothers. Leading up to the Battle of Kurukshetra, the evil Kurus cheated the Pandavas of their wealth and banished them to the forest for thirteen years.

Here we see Draupadi's husbands stripped of their finery, which is piled at the base of the dais. The hot-tempered Bhima has somehow retained a small club and is threatening an offending Kuru prince. Yudhishthira's head is bowed in shame at having gambled and lost so much.

Draupadi has been dragged by the hair into the assembly, where she is told she now belongs to the Kurus. But Draupadi is fiery, and she argues her case before the elders. No one listens. Taking their cue from their elders' silence, the younger Kurus decide to exact revenge for the slights Draupadi has inflicted on them over the years, especially her public humiliation of Karna, the adopted Kuru prince (sitting on the floor in the upper left portion of the painting.) She also laughed at the proud Duryodhana. He stands behind the throne of his blind father, **Dhritarastra,** who sits with unblinking eyes, his bearded minister by his side. Duryodhana's uncle, **Vidura,** covers his eyes in embarrassment.

The evil-looking Shakuni, mastermind of the gambling scam, sits directly below Dhritarastra. Duhshashana, Duryodhana's brother, is easily recognized by his exposed thigh. Bhima will later break that thigh during the Battle of Kurukshetra.

To truly degrade Draupadi, one of the Kurus decides to strip her. Draupadi tries to protect her honor and for a moment succeeds, but she quickly realizes she is no match for the brute tugging at her sari. She throws up her arms in surrender – not to the Kurus but to **Krishna,** her Lord. Krishna hears Draupadi's cry and comes to her rescue, appearing in the form of unending cloth. As the Kuru prince pulls, more cloth covers Draupadi. The shocked prince soon falls to the floor in exhaustion.

Draupadi's surrender is at the center of this painting. With her face made serene by spiritual release, Draupadi lifts her arms. The mystical and unseen Krishna above her supplies her with cloth. It is from this incident that Draupadi draws the strength to speak even more boldly to the Kuru elders, and it is their irreligious act toward a woman that finally drives the patience from the Pandavas' hearts and prepares them to battle their cousins.

Krishna sues for peace

Oil on canvas, 90 × 150 cm

Before the great battle between the Pandavas and the Kurus described in the famous epic, the *Mahabharata,* every attempt was made to restore peace to the kingdom. The Pandavas even requested **Krishna** – God – to mediate on their behalf. Krishna had indeed made a case for nonviolence, and it is this scene into which we are drawn in this painting.

The Pandavas were particularly inclined to find a peaceful solution to the Kurus' betrayal. The section of the *Mahabharata* in which they try to avoid war is fittingly called "The Book of Effort," and there the eldest Pandava, Yudhishthira, eloquently expresses his conviction: "War is evil in any guise. What killer is not slain in return? To those who die on the battlefield, victory and defeat are equal.... It is the righteous warriors, truly noble and with a mood of compassion, who are generally killed in war. The lesser men escape. There is naturally remorse after the killing of others, especially in the hearts of warriors who know the value of life. Only pain can come from battle."

Unfortunately, the battle between the Pandavas and the Kurus seemed unavoidable. The artist has given hints in his painting to the outcome of Krishna's appeal for peace. Heavy marble pillars and black draperies frame the palace, letting in little light. Their verticality suggests how secure the Kurus feel in their position – they are not afraid of the disenfranchised Pandavas. The black, multi-pointed star that stretches across the floor between Krishna and **Dhritarastra** juts toward the Kuru princes sitting to the side of the throne, specifically to the Pandavas' main antagonists, Duryodhana, Karna, and Duhshashana.

Although the two principal actors in this drama sit across from one another and appear to share almost equal amounts of canvas, Dhritarastra sits a little higher, but is somehow diminished in the composition. The viewer sees the scene from Krishna's standpoint.

Krishna shines with an inner light, his hand raised in the *mudra* of teaching. He did not come to beg but to instruct. Sun streams down on the king, indicating he is being offered enlightenment, but the light only seems to emphasize his sightless eyes, suggesting he is blind both physically and morally. Neither Krishna's internal light nor the sunlight shining over Dhritarastra spans the floor between them. Dhritarastra is not listening.

Krishna will close his speech to Dhritarastra with the words, "Choose the course that appears best to you." He will speak these same words again to **Arjuna** just before the battle, this time with different results.

Dhritarastra and Sanjaya

Oil on canvas, 83 × 62 cm

The blind **Dhritarastra**, father of the Kurus and the Pandavas' uncle, inquired from his secretary, the noble Sanjaya, how the Battle of Kurukshetra was progressing. Sanjaya had been empowered by his spiritual master, **Vyasa**, to see the battlefield as if he were there, so every day he conveyed everything he saw to the blind king, including the conversation **Krishna** and **Arjuna** had before the battle started, now immortalized as the *Bhagavad-gita*. Dhritarastra knew the devastating war would kill millions. He desperately prayed for his sons not to be among them.

Through Sanjaya, Dhritarastra could visualize the beautiful Krishna on Arjuna's fleet chariot. Krishna, he knew, had chosen not to fight; he served only as Arjuna's charioteer. Still, the image of the two on Arjuna's chariot distressed Dhritarastra, and we see the tension he feels as he reaches for the dagger embedded in his footstool. The filigreed hilt bears twining serpents with ruby eyes facing one another in mortal combat.

Dhritarastra said: "O Sanjaya, after my sons and the sons of Pandu assembled in the place of pilgrimage at Kurukshetra, desiring to fight, what did they do?"

Sanjaya said: "O King, after looking over the army arranged in military formation by the sons of Pandu, King Duryodhana went to his teacher and spoke the following words."

Bhagavad-gita

Bhishma on the Bed of Arrows

Oil on canvas, 90 × 57 cm

Bhishma, grandfather of the Pandava-Kuru clan, had once been the clan's crown prince, but because his father had fallen in love with a woman whose father demanded that his future grandson would sit on the throne, Bhishma relinquished his own rights and took a vow of perpetual celibacy to ensure that no one would contest his stepbrothers' claim. Because Bhishma made this gift to his father at such personal cost, the devas gave him his name, which means "one with a terrible vow." They also blessed him that he could die only by his own will.

On the tenth day of the Battle of Kurukshetra, **Arjuna** shot Bhishma full of arrows. Bhishma, however, chose not to die at that moment, so he was taken to the side of the field, where he lay wounded for nearly two months. Sages gathered around him. Bhishma, fully coherent despite his predicament, spent his last days speaking philosophy with them.

The war was over eight days later, and to please Bhishma, **Krishna** brought the Pandava brothers in all their hard-won splendor to his side. Bhishma's eyes filled with tears of joy to see his grandsons victorious after they had suffered so much.

But seeing their grandfather lying on the ground like a deva fallen from the sky, the Pandavas' hearts broke. Here we see Yudhishthira holding Bhishma's helmet and listening intently to his beloved grandfather's words of comfort and advice. Yudhishthira is paralyzed with remorse; millions of men have died to enthrone him. But Bhishma assures him that he should not be disappointed, however trying his circumstances. "In my opinion," Bhishma says, "your troubles were all due to inevitable time, under whose control everyone is carried as clouds are carried by the wind. Time is identical with Lord Krishna, and therefore its influence indicates Krishna's inexplicable wish. Don't lament things that are beyond your control."

Just after this scene, the sun's course ran into the northern hemisphere, the period most desired by mystics who die at will. Bhishma stopped speaking and fixed his attention on Krishna. The pain of his arrow wounds disappeared as his senses stopped functioning, and he prayed to his Lord, who stood beside him to bless him as he left his material body behind and entered the spiritual world. What Bhishma saw in his last meditation is depicted in the next spread.

Bhishma Remembers Krishna

Oil on canvas, 85 × 140 cm

As **Bhishma,** elder of the Pandava-Kuru clan, lay dying on a bed of arrows, his beloved **Krishna** stood next to him. Bhishma opened his eyes wide to drink in the sight and found himself caught in a memory from the battle.

This memory is described in the *Srimad-Bhagavatam,* and taking his cues from that description, the artist has painted Krishna rushing toward the powerful warrior Bhishma as he stands weaponless on his chariot, his hands open, his stance simultaneously heroic and receptive.

Krishna's rain-cloud-colored body is reflected in the blues and purples of the sky. His streaming hair is ashy from the dust raised by the horses' hoofs, and his forehead is beaded with perspiration. In his haste, his shawl drops from his shoulders.

He is in the act of breaking the promise he made not to take sides in the battle. But seeing Bhishma on the verge of killing his devotee and friend **Arjuna,** Krishna leaps from Arjuna's chariot, scoops up a broken wheel lying in the mud, and runs at Bhishma as a lion rushes an elephant.

Arjuna hastens from behind to hold Krishna back, but Krishna's hair flows out behind him as he hurries forward to protect one devotee from another while the battle rages on behind.

Bhishma allowed this vision to fill his consciousness as he prepared to leave this world. He especially appreciated Krishna's chivalrous attitude – how he protected Arjuna even in the face of Bhishma's arrows, and how he so open-heartedly came to see Bhishma on his deathbed, even though Bhishma had ill-treated him on the battlefield.

> **"May he, Lord Sri Krishna, the Personality of Godhead, who awards salvation, be my ultimate destination. On the battlefield he charged me, as if angry because of the wounds dealt by my sharp arrows. His shield was scattered, and his body was smeared with blood due to the wounds."**
>
> **Bhishma in the *Srimad-Bhagavatam***

Arjuna's Grief

Tempera on canvas, 124 × 89 cm

The *Bhagavad-gita* begins with the Pandavas and Kurus arrayed for combat. **Krishna** then pulls Arjuna's chariot into the middle of the battlefield at Arjuna's request and shows him the friends, relatives, and countrymen on both sides. Immobilized by grief, the famed bowman questions the value of a war even the winners will lose since so many lives will be lost on both sides.

This painting shows Arjuna's decision not to fight and his dropping of his celebrated Gandiva bow. Previous to this moment, Arjuna had vowed to kill anyone who even suggested he put down his bow before the battle was won, yet here he himself allows his bow to fall from his hand.

Arjuna looks down, his eyes unfocused. His body, with its sharp angles, shows no ease or direction. The background oranges and reds clash, and the pillar stretching up behind him starts on a firm base but thins as it rises, suggesting instability and uncertainty.

Krishna will now speak. In *Windows Into the Infinite: A Guide to the Hindu Scriptures,* scholar Barbara Powell gives special attention to the subject of violence and Arjuna's grief:

"Is the *Gita* advocating violence [in general]? Of course not. In many other places in the text, Krishna will extol gentleness and nonviolence, even passivity. If there's one generalization we can make about the *Gita,* it's that it embraces diversity. No one occupation, standard of conduct, or spiritual path is appropriate for everyone.... Arjuna is a *kshatriya,* a soldier by profession, and it is his moral and spiritual imperative to attend to the duties, the dharma, of that profession. Were Arjuna a priest, a spice merchant, or a housewife, Krishna would have given him very different advice, for violence is never acceptable for these people. But the question of war and peace is not the issue here at all. The issue is action and inaction. If Krishna were talking to an exhausted mother with five screaming children all needing her attention at once, she might tell him, 'Krishna, I can't face it. There's no way I can be a mom today.' His reply would be, 'Yes, you can. In fact, you must. It's your duty. Get in there and fight!' "

The battlefield context teaches us about being dutiful even in extreme situations. Most people will never find themselves facing disaster, but others, like Arjuna, do find themselves on a literal or metaphorical battlefield. The *Gita* can explain how to best react when confronted with life's hardships. Still, even as Arjuna knows he must fight and kill out of duty, he is a soft-hearted devotee of God. Naturally he is anguished by what appears to be so much senseless killing.

The Universal Form

Oil on canvas, 73 × 55 cm

While hearing the *Bhagavad-gita,* **Arjuna** was becoming enlightened, but for others' sake he wanted it known beyond a shadow of doubt that the speaker standing before him was actually God. Therefore he asked **Krishna** to prove his divinity by displaying his universal form.

If hundreds of thousands of suns were to rise at once, their radiance might resemble the effulgence of the universal form. Frightened and astonished by this vision of a God of unlimited mouths, eyes, and weapons, of the endless varieties played out in time, of all that is wondrous and frightening in existence, Arjuna folded his hands in reverence and began to pray:

"My dear Krishna, I see assembled in your body all the devas and other living beings. I see everything. Your form is difficult to behold because of its glaring effulgence spreading on all sides. That effulgence is like a blazing fire or the immeasurable radiance of the sun. I see this shining virtuosity everywhere."

Here the artist has portrayed Arjuna's vision as it is typically depicted based on the description in the *Bhagavad-gita's* eleventh chapter. Arjuna sits on his chariot and witnesses the awe-inspiring sight. He especially sees God as time. Time and death are one, and therefore many of the faces the artist has presented are threatening, weapons abound, and the material elements – earth, water, air, fire, and ether – appear as destructive rather than creative forces, even though the creator god **Brahma** rises on his lotus seat at Krishna's waist. Krishna says in the *Gita,* "Time I am, the great destroyer of the worlds, and I have come here to destroy all people." There is no escape from time or death. Still, a rainbow, symbol of hope, arcs overhead.

> **"If you think that I am able to behold your cosmic form, O my Lord, O master of all mystic power, then kindly show me that unlimited universal Self."**
>
> **Arjuna to Krishna**

The Universal Form

Oil on canvas, 116 × 140 cm

The *Bhagavad-gita* tells us **Arjuna** was given divine eyes to make the infinite universal form visible to his finite eyes. What would it be like to see everything in existence suddenly condensed into our field of vision? The previous spread shows a common depiction of that experience based on the *Bhagavad-gita's* description. Here, however, the artist uses different texts to evoke the inconceivable.

The gigantic manifestation of the phenomenal material world as a whole is God's personal body, and it's where we can experience the past, present, and future of material time. Anything material or spiritual is simply an expansion of the energy of the supreme person, whose eyes, heads, arms, and legs are everywhere. This supreme person can see, hear, touch, or appear anywhere and everywhere, for he is also the **Indweller.** His energy is all-pervasive. As a fire expands its rays and heat from a single place, so the supreme spirit expands himself through his energies everywhere and anywhere.

Yogis meditate on the universal form to help them begin to think of the supreme person's all-spiritual form. We tend to be in awe of anything powerful, whether a force of nature like destructive weather or the brute strength of a tiger or shark. The universal form encompasses all power in its source; it is the person behind nature's mask.

In this painting, to help the viewer understand the personal nature of the universe, the artist has used faces as a motif. Some of them seem emotionless, others almost Buddhistic with their half-closed eyes. Again we see Death, with his sharpened teeth and fire-breath. Bodies float up from a grave and enter Death's mouth. A cobra, symbol of **Shiva,** the great destroyer, oversees a nuclear blast. The *Srimad-Bhagavatam* tells us that earth's rivers are the veins of the gigantic universal body, the trees his hair, and the air his breath. The passing ages are his movements, and the varieties of birds his artistic sense. Human beings are his home, and the hills and mountains his bones. In this way, meditation on the universal form includes all of nature, the devas, and all dominated beings, and so incorporates all human and natural experience superimposed on a vast universal consciousness.

MAREK BUCHWALD (BARADRAJ DASA)   **1982**

The sacred song of Uddhava

Oil on canvas, 45 × 34 cm

When **Krishna's** friend and minister **Uddhava** realized that Krishna had decided to return to the spiritual world, he begged to go with him. But Krishna asked him to remain, ordering him to become a traveling monk. He then sent him to the Himalayas with a message. Before dispatching Uddhava, however, Krishna spoke a sequel to the famous *Bhagavad-gita*. This teaching is now known as the *Uddhava-gita*, "The Sacred Song of Uddhava," and it discusses everything from the nature of the material world to karma to the search for enlightenment to bhakti yoga.

At the beginning of his teachings, Krishna tells Uddhava a parable about a wandering mendicant. One day, a king met this mendicant and asked how he had become so wise, since he seemed not to be practicing any obvious spiritual disciplines. "Most people in this world live in a conflagration of lust and greed, yet you're peaceful. Where does your ecstasy come from?"

The mendicant replied that he had learned from many gurus. "From the earth I have learned tolerance and steadiness. Mountains and trees have taught me to do good for others and to live only for their benefit. My life airs move in my body without support from the outside world, and from them I have learned to be satisfied with little. From the bees who work hard only to have their honey stolen, I have learned to keep my desires simple."

The mendicant went on to name other gurus – foul air had taught him detachment; the sky had taught him that the soul, which survives all conditions, is always pure; water had taught him to keep himself clean; and cleansing fire had taught him the importance of eating pure foods. He learned from the moon that the physical body waxes and wanes, but that the self is untouched by this. By watching the sun evaporate water from the seas and rivers and return it to the earth as rain, he learned to accept gifts from others and then distribute them generously to anyone in need.

A blue-hued Krishna sits on an elevated seat, his hand in the gesture of teaching. Uddhava kneels on the floor at Krishna's feet to receive the knowledge. The sun sets behind them both. The darkness of the Age of Quarrel is approaching. Still, the lamps on either side of Krishna have already been lit. Krishna's words will light the world after his departure, and those who lose their vision because of the dense darkness of the new age will get light from his teachings to Uddhava.

uddhava

Oil on canvas, 70 × 55 cm

Uddhava is **Krishna's** cousin and minister, and in appearance, his twin, and few are as close to Krishna as Uddhava.

Just before the scene illustrated in this painting, Krishna had sent his many family members, the Yadus, to Prabhash to take a ceremonial bath so they could counteract a curse destining their dynasty to be destroyed. Having witnessed Krishna's order, Uddhava wondered why Krishna hadn't simply neutralized the curse. And then he understood: Krishna was arranging for his family members to end their stay on earth, and then he himself would depart. Uddhava was devastated.

In this painting we see Krishna sitting on the seat of a teacher. He is about to speak the *Uddhava-gita,* his last instructions to his devotee and friend, Uddhava. But first Uddhava falls at Krishna's feet and begs him not to leave him behind; the world will be too empty in his absence. Uddhava holds Krishna's feet and cries tears of love and grief. In response, Krishna, his face revealing the softness of his own heart, reaches out a hand with a dancer's gentle grace to solace his devotee. The dark folds of the curtain hanging behind Krishna and the twilight sky beyond suggest the somberness of the moment.

Krishna will not take Uddhava with him but will request him to stay for a while longer. Just as Uddhava had once carried Krishna's message to the **gopis** in Vrindavan, so Krishna will now ask Uddhava to carry a message to his devotees at Badarik Ashram in the Himalayas.

> **"Although I, the Supreme Lord, can never be captured by ordinary sense perception, those situated in human life may use their intelligence and other faculties of perception to directly search for Me through both apparent and indirectly ascertained symptoms."**
>
> **Krishna to Uddhava**
> **in the *Srimad-Bhagavatam***

Krishna and Jara

Oil on canvas, 40 × 30 cm

Having guided the Pandavas through the great *Mahabharata* war, removed his dynasty from Earth, and witnessed **Balaram's** departure for the spiritual world, **Krishna** was himself ready to end his pastimes on earth. Here he sits quietly under a pipal tree in his shining, four-armed **Vishnu** form, surrounded by the personfied forms of his mace, conch, lotus, and disc.

An aboriginal hunter bows at Krishna's feet. The hunter is Jara, and he has just shot an arrow at the reddish sole of Krishna's foot after mistaking the foot for the face of a deer. The arrow, which we see in the foreground of the painting, failed to pierce Krishna's foot because Krishna's body is spiritual, but realizing he had shot at his Lord, the hunter hurries forward to apologize.

Krishna holds his two lower hands in the *chin mudra*, a meditative hand position that represents the joining of one's consciousness with the universal consciousness. This pose indicates Krishna's imminent departure. A peacock feather rises from his crown, and his complexion, the color of a blue rain cloud, glows with the radiance of a smokeless fire, dissipating the darkness of the forest and suggesting that even in his departure, Krishna will leave his light in the world for those who wish to follow him home.

Seeing that four-armed personality, the hunter became terrified of the offense he had committed, and he fell down, placing his head upon the feet of the enemy of the demons.

Srimad-Bhagavatam

The Eyes of the Soul

Oil on canvas, 25 × 28 cm

Spiritual art, like any art, is created using both the artist's imagination and some form of matter – paint and canvas, pen and ink, stone and chisel. So what makes it "spiritual"? How do we know that the images the artist has created reflect an authentic experience of the divine?

Almost all spiritual traditions respond to this important question in a similar way. They speak of both the underlying consciousness inherent in nature and the all-pervading presence of the Oversoul, or **Indweller,** who supports everything we see. Consciousness and the Indweller have an organic relationship, which is reflected in the meeting of the world of matter with the world of spirit.

But material nature is still an imperfect copy of spirit's perfect model, so when artists draw from nature or impress its images on the form of God, there remains an inevitable coarseness to the work – something imposed by the artist's imagination. Just how much "coarseness" there is depends on how much the artist has succeeded at pushing aside his or her purely sensual impressions and allowed something truer to speak.

The Vedas call this ability to see, reflected in matter, a corresponding model of spirit, love. One text states, "I worship the primeval Lord, Govinda [**Krishna**], who is always seen by those whose eyes are anointed with the salve of love." God is situated in the heart of every atom. He is the nearest thing. How can we miss him?

True spiritual art is not the play of imagination but of soul-seeing. Whatever coarseness exists is only apparent. If we then look on the work with our own eyes anointed with love, we'll find the absolute in the relative, the positive in the negative, and spirit in matter. The spiritual form of God is an eternal truth with all its inward variety and undivided unity. What appears to us as contradiction to reason is nothing but the rules of spirit. If we look at these images with the right understanding, we'll see the full harmony in all those contradictions.

> **The spiritual form of God is an eternal truth with all its inward variety and undivided unity. What appears to us as contradiction to reason is nothing but the rules of spirit.**

sri chaitanya

In this section, we look mainly at images of Sri Chaitanya's life. Krishna's most recent avatar, Sri Chaitanya descended to inaugurate the sankirtan movement – the congregational chanting of Krishna's holy name – predicting that kirtan would spread to "every town and village" of the world.

Sri Chaitanya didn't come in the mood of God but as God's devotee, and his life was one of continuous ecstasy as he rode the waves of devotional love in a mood of separation from Krishna.

Kevin Yee (Ramadasa Abhirama Dasa)
Panca-tattva Sankirtan, 1983,
oil on canvas, 85 × 114 cm

The Heart of Devotion

Oil on board, 34 × 27 cm

The many avatars, and particularly the forms of **Radha** and **Krishna**, depicted in the previous two sections, have given rise to an elaborate tradition of devotional yoga (bhakti), often expressed through the life of **Sri Chaitanya** Mahaprabhu (1486–1533), the revered religious ecstatic who, as an avatar of Krishna appearing in the guise of his own devotee, and fully embodied the tradition's teachings and practices.

In the late fifteenth century, European kings sent explorers in search of new routes to India to bring home rich silks, exotic spices, what they considered outlandish art, and the wealth of precious gems. These kings and their merchants, however, bypassed India's real treasure, which was just then being widely distributed by Sri Chaitanya.

Just prior to Sri Chaitanya's time, a reawakening of Krishna bhakti, devotion to Krishna, was just beginning to percolate into the subcontinent, drawing largely on the Sanskrit poetry composed by Chaitanya's immediate predecessors, who themselves were drawing on the *Srimad-Bhagavatam* and other devotional texts. Now, Chaitanya and his followers were teaching spiritual aspirants how to put the deep theology these texts contained into practice, emphasizing the power of chanting Krishna's holy name.

This is not a painting of Sri Chaitanya but of his object of worship, Radha and Krishna in Vrindavan. Sri Chaitanya taught that bhakti is characterized by service. It is not a process of silent meditation, but of using body and mind to express love of God.

This mood of service is the divine nature of the soul, and Radha is the exemplar of this mood. Here, she kneels at Krishna's feet, offering flowers in worship. She gazes up at her Lord and the ultimate object of all loving service, with affection-filled eyes.

Krishna both enjoys Radha's service and desires to express his love by serving her in return. Sri Chaitanya is the embodiment of both positions – the reservoir into whom all love flows and the upwelling of that love in the form of service – the *shyam*-blue avatar of Krishna covered by the glowing gold of Radha.

Sri Chaitanya taught that bhakti is characterized by service. It is not a process of silent meditation, but of using body and mind to express love of God.

The Pancha Tattva

Oil on canvas, 111 × 73 cm

Sri Chaitanya inaugurated kirtan, the singing of God's names, as the primary means of meditation on the divine. This chanting is considered most effective when performed in the company of others, and more effective still when taken out into the streets, where others might benefit from it.

This painting depicts a yellow-dressed Sri Chaitanya stepping out of a temple and into the streets with his fellow chanters. "Pancha Tattva" literally means "five truths or features." As a combined avatar of **Radha** and **Krishna**, Sri Chaitanya is primary among those "*tattvas.*" But like a king traveling with his ministers, Sri Chaitanya does not appear alone. He comes with his four associate "*tattvas.*" First there is Nityananda, an avatar of Krishna's brother **Balaram,** seen here directly behind Sri Chaitanya with his arms upraised and his face haloed. There is also Advaita, an avatar of Mahavishu, who appears in Sri Chaitanya's pastimes as an elderly sage. He is playing the cymbals to Nityananda's right. The fourth "*tattva,*" young Gadadhara, also with upraised arms, dances meditatively in the background. He is the shakti *tattva* in Sri Chaitanya's pastimes. Next to him, with hands folded in prayer, is Srivas. Krishna descends in the form of Sri Chaitanya to play the role of his own devotee; Srivas is the embodiment of the human being who gives his life to Krishna in devotion.

Why does Sri Chaitanya appear in these five features? Although spiritually there is no difference between them, because everything on the transcendental plane is absolute, spiritual love is full of varieties. Appearing as the Pancha Tattva allows all spiritual aspirants to taste this variety as Sri Chaitanya's gift of the congregational chanting of the Hare Krishna *maha-mantra* – Hare Krishna, Hare Krishna, Krishna Krishna, Hare Hare/ Hare Rama, Hare Rama, Rama Rama, Hare Hare – lifts them beyond ritualistic forms of religion and dry meditation into accessible ecstasy.

Mark Arian (Muralidhara Dasa)
Panca-tattva Sankirtan, 1982,
oil on canvas, 85 × 114 cm

Jagai and Madhai

Oil on canvas, 70 × 100 cm

Sri Chaitanya (shown here in yellow) gave his brother Nityananda (shown here in blue) the duty to travel around the area and teach people to chant the name of God. In the town of Nadiya he came across the unruly brothers called Jagai and Madhai. These two had been born in high-caste families, but because of their association with low-class thugs, they had become drunks, meat-eaters, thieves, and arsonists. The entire town was terrified of them. Nityananda thought that if these two would embrace the chanting of the holy name, others would follow their example.

On the day Nityananda met the brothers, they were in the marketplace alternately fighting and embracing each other in their drunkenness. Nityananda watched them for a while, then decided to approach them. But he found it was not easy to sway these two. Instead of hearing what Nityananda had to say, the brothers chased him down the street, threatening to harm him if he ever returned.

Then Jagai and Madhai moved to the bank of the Ganges, near where Sri Chaitanya bathed every day. They were constantly drunk, and in that condition they harassed anyone who came to the riverside to bathe or draw water. One day, while Nityananda was walking in the dark, the brothers accosted him. They remembered him from their previous encounter, and Madhai, furious to meet him again, struck him on the forehead with a piece of broken clay pot, drawing blood. Even Jagai was shocked by the vehemence of the attack, and when his brother raised his hand again, Jagai stopped him. Witnesses were already reporting the incident to Sri Caitanya.

When Sri Chaitanya heard the news, he rushed to the spot, ready to destroy the brothers. He so dearly loved Nityananda that he could not tolerate any offense toward him. He summoned his **Vishnu** disc and prepared to lop off Madhai's head with it, as we see in the painting. The disc shines against the clouds as Sri Chaitanya holds it aloft. But Nityananda reminded Sri Chaitanya of his mission to "kill" the demons by inundating them with love of God. Nityananda also told Sri Chaitanya that Jagai had saved him from further violence. Appeased, Sri Chaitanya withdrew his disc weapon and embraced Jagai. Seeing his brother's transformation, and having just faced death, Madhai fell at Sri Chaitanya's feet and begged for his mercy.

Sri Chaitanya forgave the brothers on the condition that they use their lives more productively in the future. Both became his dedicated followers, and Madhai in particular tried to make up for his atrocious behavior by serving all those he had harassed.

Jagannath Baladeva subhadra

Acrylic on board, 44 × 28 cm

When **Sri Chaitanya** lived in Jagannath Puri, Orissa, during the last twenty-four years of his life, he worshipped a particularly ancient expression of **Krishna** known as Jagannath, or "lord of the universe". The Jagannath deity is carved in wood, and is usually seated with his brother **Balaram** and sister Subhadra, as in this painting.

In this particular depiction, black Jagannath sits below his elder brother Balaram. Below them both and protected by them is their younger sister and Jagannath's internal shakti, Subhadra. All of Krishna's avatars have two main categories of shaktis – the "internal" and the "external." Both wield the power of illusion. While the external (*maya*) shakti separates us from God through misdirection, an internal shakti like Subhadra allows us to forget God's divinity so we can increase our intimacy with him.

Jagannath's four arms and the Ananta Shesha serpents (painted green here) rising over Balaram's head clearly show that this is **Vishnu**. Although the artist has used acrylics, she has copied the brightly–colored style of a traditional pattachitra painting, a form of folk art unique to Orissa.

Lord Jagannath is an ocean of mercy and he is beautiful like a row of blackish rain clouds. He is the storehouse of bliss for Lakshmi and Saraswati, and his face is like a spotless full-blown lotus. He is worshiped by the best of demigods and sages, and his glories are sung by the Upanishads. May that Jagannath Swami be the object of my vision.

Sri Jagannathashtakam, verse 4

sage Raghunath

Oil on canvas, 77 × 59 cm

Raghunath (1495–1571), depicted here, was fifteen when he met **Sri Chaitanya**. He was born into wealth, but he so much wanted to participate in Sri Chaitanya's kirtan movement that he left home and the family business as a young man and joined Sri Chaitanya in Jagannath Puri. Sri Chaitanya and his secretary trained Raghunath in devotion, and he later became one of the six chief theologians of the Chaitanya school.

When Sri Chaitanya departed from this world, Raghunath was so grief-stricken that he decided to go to Vrindavan and end his life. First, though, he wanted to meet two of Sri Chaitanya's principal disciples, Sri Rupa and Sri Sanatan, and on his arrival in Vrindavan, these two devotees greeted him – and then convinced him to live and share with others everything he had experienced in Sri Chaitanya's presence. So each day for the next forty years, Raghunath sat and spoke about Sri Chaitanya Mahaprabhu's life and teachings.

Raghunath was famous for his severe asceticism, and here we see him in the traditional dress of a Vaishnava renunciant, holding his mendicant's water pot. This scene takes place not long after his arrival in Vrindavan.

He has just received a stone with an imprint of Sri Chaitanya's thumb. Raghunath is deeply moved by this holy relic. It soothes his heart, and encourages him to preserve his life in Sri Chaitanya's service.

Raghunath went on to write three books of poetry that illumine his profound experiences of the bhakti path. These poems and prayers encapsulate bhakti theology so completely that Raghunath was given the title "prayojan acharya", or "teacher of the highest spiritual attainment."

Rupa and Sanatan, however, did not allow him to die. They accepted him as their third brother and kept him in their company.

cleansing the Temple

Oil on canvas, 60 × 80 cm

When **Sri Chaitanya** lived in Jagannath Puri during the last twenty-four years of his life, he took part annually in the famous festival of the chariots. During the Ratha-yatra, as this festival is called, the deities of **Jagannath, Baladeva,** and **Subhadra** are taken on procession through Puri's streets. Before the procession, however, it's traditional that the deities first visit the Gundicha temple, where they are repainted over a nine-day period. Their return on the tenth day on huge carts and amid great fanfare is the Ratha-yatra festival.

In this painting we see Sri Chaitanya and his many associates preparing for the deities' arrival at Gundicha by cleaning the building's interior and exterior. After sweeping the floors, it's customary for hundreds of men to form a chain and bring water in clay pots from a nearby lake. Cleaners then throw the water over the floors, walls, ceiling, and altar, while others scrub all these surfaces. When they're finished, it is said, the temple is "as cool and pleasing as the pacified heart of God."

As Sri Chaitanya cleaned, his body gradually became covered with dust and dirt, yet he shed tears of joy. Cleansing the temple to make it fit for God's residence is nondifferent from cleansing the heart for the same purpose, and this is what Sri Chaitanya taught his followers.

Here we see Sri Chaitanya washing a temple pillar while his followers pour water on the platforms and walls. In the foreground the devotees smile; they are at ease with one another, suggesting their spirit of humility and cooperation. The devotees wear either saffron or white – the dress of renunciants or householders respectively – to suggest that Sri Chaitanya was not establishing a monastic sect, but accepted among his associates anyone who wanted to love and serve Krishna.

Cleansing the temple to make it a fit place for God's residence is nondifferent from cleansing the heart for the same purpose.

MIRIAM BRIKS (DHRITI DEVI DASI)   1983

sri chaitanya in ecstasy

Oil on canvas, 50 × 42 cm

Setting an example of what it means to be intoxicated with love of God, **Sri Chaitanya** frequently exhibited symptoms of divine madness. Often his ecstasies would lead him to lose consciousness, as depicted here.

In this painting, Sri Chaitanya has just arrived in Jagannath Puri and entered the **Jagannath** temple. The intense love for God that erupted in his heart at his first glimpse of the deity caused him to faint. The temple custodians, unsure whether he was ill or a religious charlatan, prepared to have him removed, but the king's spiritual advisor, the wise Sarvabhauma, recognized Sri Chaitanya's symptoms as devotional ecstasy and had him carried to his house. Soon after, the party that had followed Sri Chaitanya to Puri arrived and discovered his whereabouts.

A blue-clad Nityananda holds Sri Chaitanya on his lap, his body a glowing white against Chaitanya's gold. Mukunda, kneeling beside them, sings devotional songs to entice Sri Chaitanya out of his trance. Behind Mukunda we see an unknown renunciant questioning Sarvabhauma, who stands worried by the window, while Sarvabhauma's brother-in-law, Gopinath, looks on from the side, a renunciant's water pot in his hand.

Sarvabhauma Bhattacharya was very surprised to see the personal beauty of Lord Chaitanya Mahaprabhu, as well as the transcendental transformations wrought on his body due to love of Godhead.

Sri Chaitanya-charitamrita

The Passing of Haridas

Oil on canvas, 33 × 55 cm

Haridas was a Muslim who later became a **Krishna** bhakta and, through his meditation on Krishna's names, was filled with profound spiritual love. His life is an important lesson in nonsectarianism, for he is often quoted as saying, "Koran or Puran[a] – what's the difference?" His implication, of course, is that whether one is a Muslim (who reads the Koran) or a Vaishnava (who reads the *Puranas*), the soul reaches God not by sectarian affiliation but by a pure heart steeped in humility and love.

Haridas is particularly known for his commitment to japa, the private chanting of Krishna's holy names. Haridas chanted incessantly – some say 300,000 names a day – yet he still found time to help others.

He was once challenged by Maya, illusion personified, in the guise of a beautiful woman. Of course, he was too busy chanting to pay her feminine wiles much attention, and gradually his dedication inspired her to worship Krishna herself.

This painting depicts the day Haridas left this world, about two years before **Sri Chaitanya** ended his own stay. In this scene, Sri Chaitanya has lifted Haridas's lifeless body and is carrying him to the sea to prepare him for his funeral.

The painting is full of light – hardly the usual depiction of a death scene. Haridas, famed for his deep humility, seems small and contrasts with Chaitanya's complexion. A kirtan party follows and surrounds Chaitanya and Haridas in a triangular formation, with Chaitanya at the base and the Jagannath temple, seen above the trees, at the apex. The red flag, indicating that **Jagannath,** lord of the universe, is present, flies outward toward the beach. The sky around the temple is a luminous blue. Coconut palms sway in the breeze, suggesting that they too are participating in the musical glorification of Krishna's holy name.

Chaitanya dances with Haridas's body in his arms. The artist's subtle balance of lines suffuses the painting with movement and energy, suggesting the Vaishnava understanding that the death of a great soul is not to be mourned, but his return to the spiritual world celebrated.

The carefully constructed scene creates a harmony of figures centered on Sri Chaitanya, the avatar of Krishna who descended to give the congregational singing of the holy name, and Haridas, the foremost relisher of the holy name. Chaitanya's tears in the midst of his dance lend a kind of dignity to the procession.

DMYTRO SIRYI (DINABANDHU DASA)　　　　　　　　　1994

sri chaitanya's ecstasy

Oil on canvas, 69 × 50 cm

A great Vaishnava saint was once asked why the Vaishnavas say love in separation from the beloved is higher than love in union. He replied that when one's feelings of separation intensify, one comes to see the beloved everywhere, even in natural phenomena. In this way, **Radha** might mistake a tamal tree, its trunk matching the color of **Krishna's** complexion, for Krishna.

In his own ecstasy of separation from Krishna, **Sri Chaitanya** sometimes mistook ordinary objects for places of Krishna's pastimes. Once he mistook a sand dune near the ocean in Puri for **Govardhana** Hill in Vrindavan, and ran toward it, hoping to find Krishna there.

The phenomenon of love in separation is not difficult to understand because we can compare it to something we commonly experience. Consider a mother's love for her child. So engrossed is she in her child that she sees the infant wherever she looks – she beholds her child's shoe and her heart warms. This is only a crude example, but it gives us a sense of what it would be like to love God with all-consuming intensity. We would see him everywhere – and ultimately, he *is* everywhere. This is the kind of love Sri Chaitanya and his associates expressed – everything they saw was infused with Krishna and his pastimes. Ordinary girls became **gopis** and commonplace geography became the sacred places of Krishna's divine pastimes.

In this painting, Sri Chaitanya confuses the Indian Ocean with the **Yamuna River.** Here we see him plunging into the ocean, his face infused with spiritual expectation, calling out Krishna's names. His body lifts above the horizon, suggesting the transcendence of his experience. His aura brightens the clouds that begin to glow and take up the movement of the wave.

> **Brightened by the shining light of the moon, the high waves of the sea glittered like the waters of the river Yamuna. Mistaking the sea for the Yamuna, the Lord ran swiftly and jumped into the water, unseen by the others.**
>
> *Sri Chaitanya-charitamrita*

Three Avatars in One

Oil on canvas, 76 × 46 cm

Sri Chaitanya sometimes revealed his other avatar forms to certain of his devotees. Srivas, who himself was an avatar of the sage **Narada,** once saw Sri Chaitanya as **Vishnu.** Chaitanya showed both his boar incarnation and his form as **Rama** to a devotee named Murari. He appeared as flute-playing **Krishna** to his mother, as **Radha** and Krishna to Ramananda, and as the **universal form** to Advaita.

He showed his six-armed form (*shadbhuj*) twice – once to Nityananda and another time to Sarvabhauma, the local king's royal philosopher. The six-armed form is not a single avatar but three forms in one. The green-skinned Rama carries a bow and arrow; blue Krishna plays the flute; and Sri Chaitanya himself carries the traditional water pot and staff of a renunciant.

Because the Chaitanya avatar was posing as a devotee, he hid his divinity from his followers. So it was significant that he revealed this six-armed form. Sri Chaitanya's followers were mainly worshipers of either Rama or Krishna. In showing three avatars in one, he proved his nondifference from these other forms of the Godhead, and also showed the devotees the oneness of Rama and Krishna. All three avatars – Chaitanya, Krishna, and Rama – are the same person appearing in different moods.

Although Sri Chaitanya revealed his six-armed form in Jagannath Puri, the artist has painted a Vrindavan background, with the **Yamuna** River flowing through the scene and a peacock craning its neck from a low branch. All holy places encourage particular types of remembrance of God, and Jagannath Puri is a place for remembrance in a mood of separation. Therefore the artist has painted his *shadbhuj* with a golden-complexioned face – but it is not Sri Chaitanya's face, as we would expect; it is a golden Krishna, complete with crown and peacock feather.

Judy Koslofsky (Jadurani Devi Dasi)
Shad-bhuj, 1974,
oil on canvas, 57 × 43 cm

The Artists

ARAM MELKONIAN
Born 1961 in Yerevan, Armenia
Living in California, USA

DENNIS SIRRINE
(DHRUVA MAHARAJA DASA)
Born 1947 in Michigan, USA
Living in Connecticut, USA

DEVAHUTI DEVI DASI
Born in the USA.

DMYTRO SIRYI
(DINABANDHU DASA)
Born 1972 in Kharkov, Ukraine
Living in Auckland, New Zealand

DOMINIQUE AMENDOLA
(DRIGHA DEVI DASI)
Born 1950 in Paris, France
Living in Vermont, USA

DOUG BALL (PARIKSIT DASA)
Born 1950 in Colorado, USA
Living in Hawaii, USA

GIAMPAOLO TOMASSETTI
(JÑANANJANA DASA)
Born 1955 in Terni, Italy
Living in Città di Castello, Italy

KAREN DAY
(GUNDICHA DEVI DASI)
Born 1989 in Pennsylvania, USA
Living in California, USA

HANS OLSON
Born 1955 in Iowa, USA
Living in Iowa, USA

JANETTE TOMBLESON
(JAGAT KARANA DEVI DASI)
Born 1951 in Newcastle, NSW, Australia
Living in Sydney, Australia

JESPER WERNEBURG
(JAHNUDVIPA DASA)
Born 1956 in Copenhagen, Denmark
Living in Mayapur, W.B., India

JÜRGEN WILMS
(AJATASHATRU DASA)
Born 1951 in Germany
Living in New Mexico, USA

JOHANNES PTOK
(JANMANALAYA DASA)
Born 1950 in Berlin, Germany
Living in Järna, Sweden

JUDY KOSLOFSKY
(JADURANI DEVI DASI)
Born 1947 in New York, USA
Living in Vrindavan, U.P., India

KALIYEV EDIK
(SACCIDANANDA DASA)
Born 1957 in Almaty, Kazakhstan
Living in Vrindavan, U.P., India

SERGEJ IVOCHKIN
(KEVALA BHAKTI DASA)
Born 1975 in Moscow, Russia
Living in Moscow, Russia

KEVIN YEE
(RAMADASA ABHIRAMA DASA)
Born 1951 in Hawaii, USA
Living in California, USA

LUISA NUNZIATI
(PREMAVILASA DEVI DASI)
Born 1953 in Rome, Italy
Living in Città di Castello, Italy

MAREK BUCHWALD
(BARADRAJ DASA)
Born 1946 in Tashkent, Uzbekistan
Living in California, USA

MARK ARIAN
(MURALIDHARA DASA)
Born 1947 in Iowa, USA
Living in California, USA

MATTHEW GOLDMAN
(PUSKAR DASA)
Born 1947 in New York, USA
Living in Florida, USA

MIRIAM BRIKS
(DHRITI DEVI DASI)
Born 1958 in Wrocław, Poland
Living in California, USA

PIETRO DI GIOVANNANTONIO
(PRASANTA DASA)
Born 1957 in Rome, Italy
Living in Tavarnelle Val di Pesa, Italy

RAM ROJAS
(RAMANATHA DASA)
Born 1955 in Caracas, Venezuela
Living in Wisconsin, USA

ROSS GOODE
(RAMAPRASAD DASA)
Born 1951 in Australia
Living in Murwillumbah, NSW, Australia

SALVATORE DI FOGGIA
(SUDDHA BHAKTA DASA)
Born in Italy.

VLAD HOLST
(VASUPRIYA DASA)
Born 1972 in Magnitogorsk, Russia
Living in Moscow, Russia

Readers interested in the subject matter of this book are invited to contact one of the following information centers:

United Kingdom
+44 1923 857244   readerservices@pamho.net

United States
+1 800 927 4152   bbt.usa@krishna.com

Other Countries
+32 86 323280   bls@pamho.net

Produced and published by
The Bhaktivedanta Book Trust
Korsnäs Gård, 14792 Grödinge, Sweden

www.bbt.se
www.bbtmedia.com
www.bbt.org
www.krishna.com

Steven J. Rosen (Satyaraja Dasa) is a disciple of His Divine Grace A. C. Bhaktivedanta Swami Prabhupada and author of some thirty books in the fields of philosophy, history, spirituality, and music, including the popular *Hidden Glory of India.* He is associate editor of *Back to Godhead* magazine, as well as founding editor of *The Journal of Vaishnava Studies.* He lives in New York, USA.

MIX
Paper from
responsible sources
FSC
www.fsc.org   FSC® C083411

ISBN 978-91-7149-801-4
Printed in May 2016

Cover: **Johannes Ptok** (Janmanalaya Dasa)
Narasingha (detail)
See the full painting on page 54.

Page 1: **Johannes Ptok** (Janmanalaya Dasa)
The Universal Form (detail)
See the full painting on page 191.

Page 2: **Ross Goode** (Ramaprasad Dasa)
Rama Kills Ravana, oil on canvas, 54 × 41 cm

Kaisori Bellach has studied bhakti yoga for almost forty years, with an abiding interest in its cultural expression through writing, music, and the fine arts. She has worked as an editor for almost as many years, first as a freelance editor, and then with an independent publishing house. She lives in Ohio, USA, and works for the Bhaktivedanta Book Trust.